I0605941

PRAISE FOR

The SOIL *of* LEADERSHIP

"Britt weaves over twenty-five years of global leadership experience with sustainable farming insights. It's an invitation to consider an emergent, humble leadership approach for a thriving future."

MATT KOLAN, PhD, director, University of Vermont Leadership for Sustainability (MLS) and Transdisciplinary Leadership and Creativity for Sustainability (TLCS)

"A must-read for leaders facing a crisis of leadership and connection. Britt offers a way forward with practical tools for building and inspiring community action."

MARIKO SILVER, PhD, president and CEO, Henry Luce Foundation

"*The Soil of Leadership* is a fresh contribution to leadership literature, employing metaphor to reflect on sustainable practices. Rich with diverse insights, it's recommended for transformative leadership."

ANN DOWNER, EdD, professor emeritus, University of Washington Department of Global Health, School of Public Health and Community Medicine

"A touching reminder of essential leadership values, this book uses the soil metaphor to highlight growth, balance, and self-peace. It encourages readers to reflect, heal, and grow in their leadership journey, enhanced by Britt's insightful leadership sessions."

FRED BAUMA, human rights activist

"Dr. Yamamoto's 'Leadership 3.0' presents a new, exciting framework for leadership development. It's a transformative resource, enriching and inspiring leaders across disciplines with its focus on reflection, wellbeing, and awareness."

DAVID L. KIM, senior director for leadership and exchanges programs, The Asia Foundation

"*The Soil of Leadership* is a crucial resource for those working toward social change. Britt Yamamoto expertly intertwines global leadership principles with a deep connection to the earth, offering practical methods for building a culture of connected leadership."

LINA SRIVASTAVA, founder, Center for Transformational Change

"Britt Yamamoto's *The Soil of Leadership* invites leaders to return to earth-connected strategies, moving beyond linear, heroic approaches. It challenges us to pay attention to the small, incremental ways we can enact change and honor the sacred in our leadership practices."

JENNIFER LENTFER, leadership coach and communication strategist

"This book transforms implicit wisdom into explicit tools, significantly impacting social innovators' work and lives. Its use of experiential metaphors provides a grounding and inspiring perspective, essential for leadership development."

HIDEYUKI AND YUKI INOUE, cofounders, INNO-Lab International

www.amplifypublishinggroup.com

The Soil of Leadership: Cultivating the Conditions for Transformation

For more information, please contact:
Amplify Publishing, an imprint of Amplify Publishing Group
620 Herndon Parkway, Suite 220
Herndon, VA 20170
info@amplifypublishing.com

Library of Congress Control Number: 2023923700

CPSIA Code: PRV0324A

ISBN-13: 979-8-89138-055-4

Printed in the United States

To Dr. Takekuma, whose wisdom, guidance,
and sense of humor continue to shape my path.

The SOIL *of* LEADERSHIP

Cultivating *the* Conditions *for* Transformation

DR. BRITT YAMAMOTO

CONTENTS

INTRODUCTION

For over twenty-five years, I have had the good fortune to work closely with leaders of all ages and a wide range of experience, from across sectors and all over the world. Through my years of facilitating intensive leadership trainings, designing programs, and advising and coaching executives, I have traced a thread that knits together the work of leadership: whether running a hospital in Uganda, shaping vocational training in Vietnam, campaigning for office in Iraqi Kurdistan, managing donor relations in Boston, or movement building in Nicaragua.

We seek connection.

We seek greater connection to ourselves, our communities, our work, our place in the world, yet these very same contexts are usually rife with disconnections, forces that drive us away and push us apart.

This is a book about a leadership practice that works to unify and connect.

We are so often told that the task of leaders is to coerce and influence. But the real work of leadership is to inspire and enact connection and, as a result, animate what educator Parker Palmer calls the "hidden wholeness" that lives within each of us, our work, and our communities.

And so this book is ultimately for those—whether they identify as a leader or not—who seek a greater connection to themselves, their work, and perhaps their place in the world.

My hope is that this journey will result in greater clarity on how you approach your leadership. And we will get there, not through the realm of the extraordinary, but by developing a new framework for understanding the familiar and ordinary, the largely unconscious patterns, behaviors, and assumptions that accumulate and shape our being.

One of the most important lessons of my life has been that transformational learning can, and perhaps should, be as much about new perspectives reshaping an understanding of the familiar, as an exploration of the previously unknown. Your most important journeys need not trace the arc of a prolonged hero's quest, but rather can focus most fruitfully on what is right beneath your feet. This is why I will invite you to place your hands into the soil that supports and nurtures you, so you can learn to see anew what is under the familiar ground on which you walk.

Put another way, let's dig where we stand.

TOOLS FOR GROWTH

The Soil of Leadership approach emerges primarily from my work over the past two decades with leaders based in Latin America, the Asia-Pacific region, Africa, and North America and working in the social sector, but it is a methodology that is applicable across sectors and industries. I have found that its core principles resonate with anyone who seeks a deeper connection to themselves and their work.

This book will provide practical tools to help orient you toward implementing a leadership that unifies and connects, while sharing the stories and practical experience of leaders who transformed their relationships with their work, their teams, and themselves through this approach to leadership development and greater self-awareness.

I came to the work of leadership through my experience as a farmer, social entrepreneur, and professor. Natural systems and our relationship to them taught me so much about how to become a more connected leader; they also have become my most powerful teaching framework to help others to become more connected leaders as well. In these pages I share with you some of the most significant leadership lessons I absorbed while learning to be a sustainable farmer and organizational leader.

Despite the best efforts of the "leadership development field" to point you to clear binaries of "good" or "bad" (even "best"), such binaries emphasize shortcuts and coping mechanisms that can lead to poor decisions and hubris. Leading is contextual, inquiry-based work that requires an awareness of self and surroundings and how the unique configuration is held together by the seen and unseen—that which is both above and below the surface. It requires breaking through old binaries and our tendencies to seek simple solutions.

So many of the leadership and management ideas presented to us as skills actually are little more than coping mechanisms, aimed at getting you through (or past) challenging points as quickly as possible so you can produce more efficiently, or just more quickly. These are not, in my estimation, true skills. They are certainly not skills for growth that will help you become a more capable, fulfilled, generative, and inspired leader. The tools I share here have helped leaders transform their perspectives in ways that unleash a deeper reserve of creative and generative potential.

This is what we will do together.

Slow and Spacious

As you engage the material, some insights may come with a flash of clarity, while others may take some time before the learning bears fruit. If there are times when you need to stop, reflect, and perhaps even take space and distance yourself from the material, you are always welcome. In fact, I hope that in reading you embrace a slower cadence, so that what you learn can be as purposeful and relevant as possible.

Be mindful to breathe as you read.

So, if and when you find yourself curious, questioning, challenged, or just plain in disagreement about what you find in this book, you are where you need to be. The key is that you use that opportunity to turn toward the roots of these beliefs and perceptions and, in working to find a closer connection, find greater clarity. Harvest what nourishes you now, and trust the invitation to reengage at your own pace with whatever you leave behind.

While I use farming stories and metaphors, this is not a how-to manual for becoming a sustainable farmer, neither is it a how-to for becoming a specific type of leader: there's no such thing as the right kind of sustainable farmer; there are only basic shared principles. Everything else that happens on a farm is as unique as the farmer, their land, their community, and the purpose that binds them together. So, too, is it with leadership.

In the same way that our contemporary relationship with agriculture needs to move from a commercial, conventional farming (focused on a science-based approach to managing plants) to a commercial, organic farming (focused on nurturing healthy plants), to eventually a community-based, sustainable, and regenerative farming (focused on building healthy soil), so, too, do I see how we need to be taking a fundamentally new approach when it comes to leadership development.

Evolving Leadership Development

I have come to see leadership development programs as part of an evolutionary arc that is just beginning to recognize the need for leadership to grow and be tended to from the inside out.

Starting from the inside and moving out facilitates a transformative process. It allows leaders to reconnect to their vision and purpose, find their renewal, tend to their well-being, and ultimately lead from a place of greater awareness. I call this approach to leadership development Leadership 3.0.

3.0: Cultivating the Inner World of Leadership

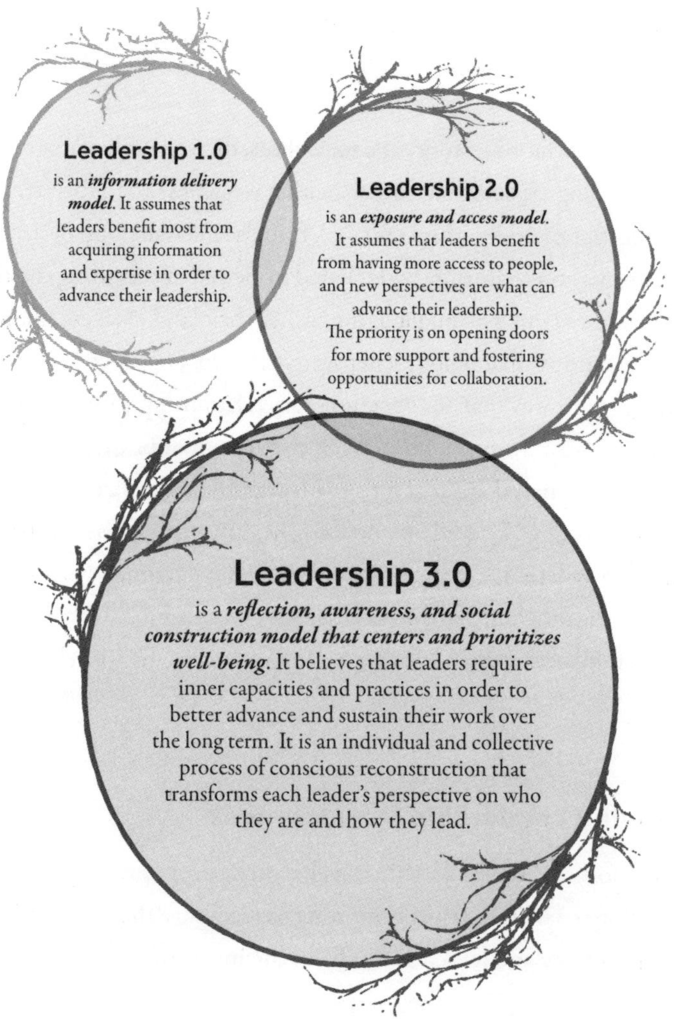

Leadership 1.0

Leadership 1.0 is a product of traditional education methodologies where a teacher (the expert) provides the student (a trainee) with information that presumably will help to advance their lives. This typically shows up in training programs that build organizational management skills such as supervision, board development, fundraising, etc. More recently, it shows up in the popularity of internet-ready communication strategies such as fast pitching, TED-style talks, etc.

One of the biggest shortcomings in the Leadership 1.0 approach is that it offers a mechanistic approach to leadership development, providing leaders with specific skills that are more about managing an organization than leading systemic change and largely ignoring the stories on which they are built.

Leadership 2.0

Moving away from the received learning approach of Leadership 1.0, the 2.0 approach to learning recognizes the importance of networks and human relationships to advance social change and prioritizes experience and exposure. Activities like site visits, forums, conferences, and study tours give participants new perspectives on their lives and opportunities to share and bond with others whom they may not otherwise have the chance to meet. These new perspectives and relationships are valuable human and social capital for leaders to use to advance their work.

Without a well-designed, intentional learning structure to help process these experiences, participants can struggle to make meaning from these opportunities. In fact, the most important skill is not making the connections, but knowing how to sift through them, and discerning what is most useful.

Leadership 3.0

Leadership 3.0 draws upon the most useful aspects of 1.0 and 2.0 and grounds a leader's growth in their lived reality. The most transformational work is at the intersection of retreat and engagement. When leaders are able to name, articulate, and reframe their realities, it opens up a new awareness that is powerful and life changing. This generative force produces leaders who are inspired and reconnected to what matters.

Often Leadership 1.0 is referred to as teaching *hard skills,* while the Leadership 3.0 focus is on *soft skills.* My experience, however, is that this framework is inaccurate at best and deceptive at worst. Anyone who has gone through the rigorous process of an honest engagement with questions like *Who am I?* and *Why do I do what I do?* knows that it is very hard! Therefore, I propose that the hard-soft framing be changed to easy-hard or transactional-transformational. No matter how you frame the difference, Leadership 3.0 gives leaders the capacity to maximize the skills gained through Leadership 1.0 and 2.0.

Needless to say, the Soil of Leadership is firmly rooted in Leadership 3.0.

In my life and leadership, I know I am at my best when I feel deeply rooted in a well-tended foundation of purpose. I am more creative, make better decisions, and find myself more often in a state of flow. These are the times when I have founded and built companies, taught and inspired students, run seven marathons in seven months, and farmed and fed thousands of people.

But the throughline of all that diverse work is simple: your fruits are only as strong as your roots.

How do you cultivate the conditions for transformation in your workplace, your community, your leadership, your life?

There is knowledge and insight to be gleaned from looking to the plants.

But the deeper wisdom is found in the soil.

Let's discover the Soil of Leadership.

CHAPTER 1

The Trip from Dirt to Soil

Richness of the tilth,
all that is metabolized,
a promise of life.

Soil is dirt transformed.

Before I learned how to farm, I didn't know the difference.

I could take a handful of earth, but it held no real meaning to me. I had no relationship with it nor connection to it.

It was just a pile of dirt.

Dirt was a holding mechanism, inert and largely a nuisance. In common parlance, its closest associations are likely to be dirty, unclean, unseemly, even existing outside of the socially acceptable realm. It is not so much the substance of life, but perhaps even the opposite, more adjacent to soot and dust, four-letter kin that speak to a natural process at the end of its life cycle. Dirt smells of abandonment and loss. It clouds your eyes, invades your space, and robs the moisture from your skin. It tastes like dirt.

Or so I thought before I became a farmer.

Before I learned how to place my hands in the earth and connect to the soil.

MY ROOTS

There is nothing quite like a sustainable farm in early October.

Walking the pathways, feeling the loamy earth beneath your feet, the experience greets all five senses with such immediacy that you'd be forgiven if you could not untangle the sights, smells, sounds, and the anticipation of taste. Sweet peas adventuring beyond the edge of their trellis. Flowers and bees in heated exchange. Plump, sun-kissed tomatoes with bursts of flavor that defy restraint. Daikon radishes inviting you to grab their gently spiked leaves to see what lies beneath.

Amidst the vibrancy, the understanding that everything is now at its fullest: at the edge of growth and decline, a magical moment when the things around you reflect all that life is, the brilliance inseparable from its impending muting.

I am a *yonsei,* a fourth-generation Japanese American, and while I was born in Japan, my American parents returned with me to the United States only a few months after my birth. I then grew up in a small beach community in southern California, where I spent much of my childhood playing in the surf or in the surrounding foothills of coastal sage scrub.

Growing up in a predominantly white community as one of only a handful of Asian American/Pacific Islanders, I developed a complicated and sometimes fraught relationship to my presenting identity and, more specifically, to Japan. I held that part of me at arm's length and actively turned away from behaviors and activities, such as speaking Japanese, that I believed would affirm my difference from those around me.

In college, I began to explore more fully and to understand my story and how my personal experience was shaped by so much more than I had previously imagined, including my "Japaneseness." I felt this turn so acutely that I focused my studies on Asian American literature and history, and when I graduated, I was set on becoming a professor of Asian American studies. As a result of that time period, I would come to better understand issues of inclusion and exclusion, identity formation, and how history and power shape cultural norms.

But for all my personal growth, I still had no interest in Japan. After college I traveled internationally as much as I could—from Italy to Nicaragua to India, but I felt no pull to visit Japan. As a place, it remained, in my heart and mind, as remote as ever.

It was not until I developed an interest in farming and the intersection between food and community building that I would chart a route to find my roots.

THE ARRIVAL

"Dr. Takekuma. Teaches sustainable farming. Work/study available."

That was the entry in a small callout box for "Environmental Organizations in Japan" buried deep in the Moon Publishing Japan travel guidebook I was perusing in the bookstore. The only additional information was a mailing address and fax number, so I sent off a fax (!) inquiring about any opportunities on the farm and waited.

A month would pass before I received a voicemail saying that Dr. Takekuma warmly welcomed me to live, work, and learn on the farm. Because I was still fully in "backpacker mode," within a few weeks I was on a plane to Japan, the place where I was born, but had never been.

My first sleep at the farm was a very short one. I had arrived in the rural village around midnight after a long bus ride from the municipal airport that capped off nearly twenty-four hours in transit. Because, at that time, I did not speak any Japanese and Dr. Takekuma's farm was in a rural area, it was only through a series of gestures and preprinted documents with Japanese writing that I even made it that far.

I will never forget the moment the driver slowed the bus, pointed at me and then to the doors, indicating that this was my stop. I exited to a dim streetlight, prominent vending machine, and a sea of darkness. All I could do was wait. After what seemed like an hour, but was likely ten minutes, a small truck pulled up, and it was my ride. I was taken to a futon and told to please be up by 6:00 a.m.

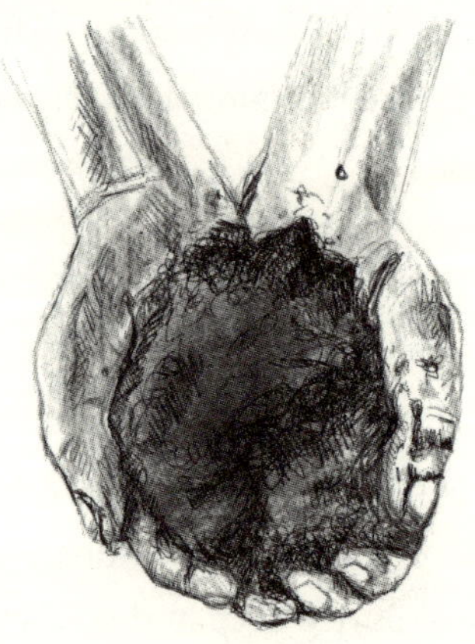

Indeed, by 4:30 a.m. I was up and wide-eyed with jetlag and anticipation. Poised and ready with my quick-dry pants, layers of light cotton, Timberland boots, and baseball cap, I felt prepared (or at least dressed) for anything from a brisk morning walk to watch the sunrise over the Sierra Nevada to saving humanity through sustainable farming.

But before I could take step one, I bumped up against the enormity of what I did not know.

The room where I would live for the next year was in a very traditional Japanese farmhouse with a mixture of dirt floors, tatami rooms, vaulted ceilings with exposed beams, and sliding shoji doors—lots of them.

At 5:45 a.m. I was just one set of shoji away from my first day on the job—but I didn't even know how to get out of my room. With frustration and outsized, clamoring effort, I wrestled my lumbering form through the paper-and-wood sliding door. Yet I wasn't even self-aware enough to read a lesson into my own clumsiness. It was only when I finally managed to take a deep breath and gently slide the door open and closed, that I began to gauge the steep learning curve that lay ahead. Along that curve I would be forced to reconsider everything I thought I knew, beginning with the first step: how to cross a threshold.

On the other side of the last set of doors were my new coworkers. The fact that they didn't burst out laughing at the sight of me, with my clumsiness and comical getup, was early proof of their enormous kindness and patience.

Without much more than a shared glance, my hosts offered a change of clothes: khaki polyester pants with matching jacket and rubber boots, a more befitting uniform for a farmer in Japan.

Immediately, I was both at home and deeply out of place.

GROWING SOIL

Dr. Takekuma had walked me out of the farmhouse and into the nearest field, a relatively small two acres, teeming with color and life. He turned to me and asked:

"What is the difference between a conventional farmer and a sustainable farmer?"

This question would change the trajectory of my life.

My grandparents were farmers, but I did not grow up knowing or experiencing agriculture in this way. They wanted something else for me, but I was drawn to the land. I was there because I had decided: I want to learn how to renew community through agriculture.

Prior to leaving for Japan, I had read every book or article I could find, devouring the writing and philosophies of such people as Vandana Shiva, Bill Mollison, Rachel Carson, and J. I. Rodale.

So, when Dr. Takekuma asked, I was sure I was ready. I had studied for this exam question! I stood up straighter. Rocky start be damned, it was time for redemption.

I was certain I knew the answer and could impress him. The only issue was where to begin.

I could say that the conventional farmer prioritizes production—rows of grains farther than the eye can see and more than the mono-cropped field can stand—while the sustainable farmer leans into biodiversity, helping the land help itself.

I could contrast the pest-killing chemicals stocked in the conventional farmer's toolkit with the natural amendments on which the sustainable farmer draws in order to foster an ecosystem in which each member nourishes one another in succession.

Or perhaps enumerate the ways conventional farmers exacerbate climate change while sustainable farmers tread as lightly on the surface of the earth as any humans.

Or maybe explain how sustainable farmers prioritize local and community markets while conventional farmers prioritize global and commercial ones.

Eager to prove my bona fides, I dove deep into what I believed were all the right answers.

When I came up for air, I searched his face for a sign of approval.

Waiting until he was sure I had finished speaking, he said to me, "All of those things may or may not be correct. But what you need to know is that the main difference between a conventional farmer and a sustainable farmer is this: the conventional farmer grows plants, and the sustainable farmer grows soil."

My reactive and critical mind wanted to restate the sentence with adjectives and adverbs dripping with judgment that would impugn the techniques, motives, and yields of the conventional farmer and laud the wisdom, inspiration, and bounty of the sustainable farmer.

But, more than anything, I was disarmed by the simplicity of what he had said.

Through my months on the farm sowing seeds, thinning starts, weeding beds, and harvesting crops, I had many occasions to turn the juxtaposition over in my mind.

The conventional farmer grows plants.

True enough. Any child knows that farmers grow plants. That's where fruits and vegetables come from, in our collective imagination.

It's only when we continue on and consider the second proposition that things get interesting.

The sustainable farmer grows soil.

A provocation—or artistic license? Soil doesn't *grow;* soil sits there and receives seeds, water, and nutrients so that plants grow *in it.* A holding mechanism. As generative as a shopping cart.

Caught up in images of picture-book farmers standing shoulder to shoulder with breezy stalks of grain, their hands bursting with bunches of leafy greens, we've never learned to train our gaze downward, in between the sprouts and stalks and shoots destined to become our next meal. As tomatoes and cucumbers and squash make their seasonal appearance, the loamy, deep brown, very-much-alive soil *grows*—season after season—the gracious host for all the guests invited to join in the fun of taking root.

Put the two sentences back together, and their divergent temporalities come to the fore: the conventional farmer grows plants, their success measured by their seasonal yield; the sustainable farmer grows soil over the course of years, prioritizing its long-term health over any expectation of a specific harvest.

The former focuses on the short term and what can be seen above the surface, while the latter is invested in the future and what lies beneath, obscured from view.

PLANT-BASED VS. SOIL-BASED

Dr. Takekuma's words inducted me into a practice of sustainable farming that would consume me over the next decade of my life, including starting a certified organic farm of my own on an abandoned lot in Southern California. But what I did not realize at the time was that in this reframing of my thoughts on agriculture, I was also undergoing a profound reorganization of my worldview. Only now can I look back and recognize that, since that moment, my life's work has been shaped by the central theme of cultivating the conditions for transformation.

While this was literally apparent during my time as a full-time farmer, I also saw *plant-based* propositions everywhere I went throughout my academic training and work as a social entrepreneur, whether it was in an office, a seminar room, or sleeves rolled up in a startup business or nonprofit: managers, leaders, teachers all trying to get output from the things they could see. How to increase performance. How to improve metrics. How to boost satisfaction.

At the same time, the kinds of *soil-based* inquiries that offer more depth and meaning—such as how to build trust and connection between people—are discounted as "soft," with little awareness of the kind of commitment and resources necessary to achieve them.

Even in fields whose watchwords are long-term growth and development, such as leadership and international education (another place where I've made my home), this problem is widespread. In the early days of building one of my organizations focused on leadership development for young adults, I remember being in conversation with the executive director of a larger organization who boasted of how many young, emerging leaders they were rapidly pumping through their programs. When I asked what kind of consideration was being given to how these young leaders could integrate their learning so that it did not end up being a parenthetical experience, he responded, "That's not our problem to solve."

How shortsighted a farmer would be to cultivate trays of seeds without the least concern with where they would be transplanted once they outgrew their plastic birthplace! And yet that is where the conventional leadership training stopped. If the young leaders represent seedlings—and it's no stretch, given the leadership world's infatuation with germination metaphors—these programs were limiting their potential by not helping them to grow rich soil.

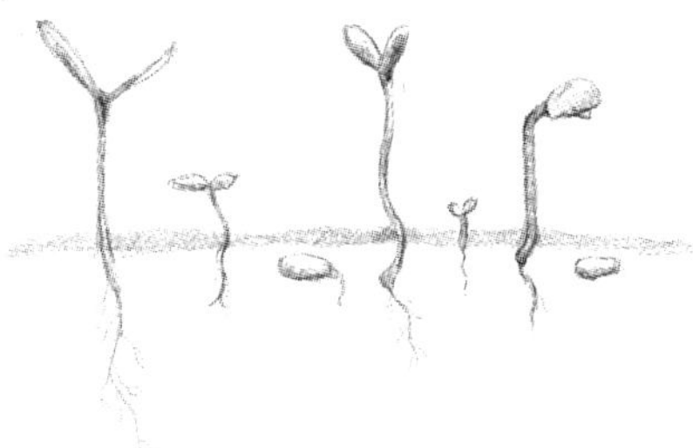

But this metaphor isn't just about making sure new leaders have a place to thrive in their next phase. Without attention to the soil, you'll only ever yield anything of significance by continuously propping up your languishing seedlings, running on a treadmill to keep them pumped full of compensatory, external inputs. Essentially a recipe for discontent, misalignment, disconnection, and burnout.

Anyone who has ever spent much time in any organization knows what I mean. There's a challenge, an obstacle, an agenda that urgently needs addressing. It's probably been called to the management's attention because of some kind of crisis (or poor results from some monitoring and evaluation study), and someone decides that the solution is more inclusivity, trust-building, or communication skills. A workshop is held—offering tools, processes, and best practices. Everyone agrees they're important, tries their best to follow instructions, and says the right things in response to the prompts.

Maybe you yield a quick harvest: improved satisfaction scores, faster turn-around time. But not long after the worksheets are in the recycle bin, everything withers away. "Remember when we did that trust building exercise? Whatever happened to that . . . ?"

What *happened* is rarely malevolent. You can plant the most carefully chosen seeds, in the right season, according to the exact specifications of depth and spacing, but if your soil has been fumigated within an inch of its life, you've got a long road—what the organic certification process calls remediation—before you'll ever taste the fruits of your labor.

In other words, if you don't cultivate the conditions, investing in the long-term transformation of the soil, nothing will ever fully take root. Growing plants without an attention to the soil is to ignore the fullness and complexity of what it takes to steward life.

In leadership, a narrow focus on the things we can see and measure can prevent us from more truly understanding what is happening in and around us, and we lose sight of the long-view work of building lasting systems and processes. And even in the short view, we may be missing important information that is right in front of us, like thoughtlessly pulling weeds from our fields without taking the time to look beyond our assumptions and ask what the presence of these weeds is telling us in the first place.

Organizations and businesses usually need to have conventional, output-oriented goals: performance, measurement, and accountability are all very real things. But if those goals, and the approach to work, focus only on that which we can see—plant-based, above-the-ground strategies—we will struggle to build the kinds of symbiotic connections between individuals or groups that provide shared context and generate the conditions for growth. In order to make change together, we must invest in building soil together, so that we can imagine what we cannot yet see.

But to be clear, sustainable farmers cannot simply grow soil and focus on cultivating the conditions for growth and transformation on their farms. These conditions must also produce things—if not for economic generation, then for the sustenance and well-being of others. After all, we carefully cultivate the conditions so that we can produce healthy plants. So it is very much a *both/and* (both plants *and* soil), not an *either/or* (either plants *or* soil). Unfortunately, most approaches—whether they are literal (farming) or metaphorical (leadership)—are heavily skewed toward plants and that which can be immediately seen and known.

Cultivating the Conditions in Latin America

"I oversee the management of nine homes for disadvantaged and vulnerable children, youth, families, and communities across Latin America and the Caribbean. Being the executive director, I have to be focused on the output—ensuring that there are enough funds and resources to run the homes and community programs, while also making sure the management team is operating smoothly and at full capacity. I also have to make sure all program activities operate consistently and ethically within NPH's mission, values, and policies.

As time went on, I began to observe that I was only being informed about certain issues pertaining to HR and management once things got out of hand. While I assumed I had given my staff plenty of opportunities to talk to me about certain situations, the sharing was not happening at the level that I wanted. As I reflected on the staff meetings and the way I was conducting them, I soon came to realize that my approach was a "plant-based proposition." With that realization, I began to create time and space for cultivating the conditions—so that I could focus on both the soil and the plant. Our meetings and interactions are far different as we first seek connection and relationship, as hard as that might be."

Miguel Venegas (Mexico)
Executive Director
Nuestros Pequeños Hermanos International

Cultivating the Conditions in South Asia

"My leadership role presents unique challenges; one of the most formidable aspects is bringing together diverse groups and stakeholders to develop a collective stance on education policy processes. This involves fostering dialogue, building bridges, and ensuring all voices are heard. Additionally, motivating my team amidst the slow pace of public policy and behavioral change, while shirking spaces for civil society, presents ongoing challenges. In the face of these obstacles, the concept of soil building has transformed the way that I approach my work. It has shifted the primary focus away from short-term vision and immediate outputs and opened my frame to prioritize the underlying systemic challenges that hinder access to education for marginalized children, such as gender inequality, social barriers, and resource constraints. While it may seem only conceptual, this framework has changed the way that I see my work and what I need to be focused on to pursue my vision."

Kaneez Zehra (Pakistan)
National Coordinator, Pakistan Coalition for Education
Executive Director, Society for Access to Quality Education

REFLECTION

As you complete this chapter, I invite you to take a moment to pause and reflect. Remember, there is no right or wrong, simply observing and taking note:

- Take a look back at the last week, or month, of your calendar. How much of your time was spent on plant-based vs. soil-based activities at work? With family and friends?
- Think about how you measure success within your organization and for yourself. Are you mostly considering plant-based (near-term) or soil-based (long-term) metrics and assessments?
- When you think about your plant-based endeavors, how do you feel?
- When you think about your soil-based endeavors, how do you feel?

CHAPTER 2

Soil Building

Our lives, like the seasons,
turn from light into darkness.
The warmth of the sun
shrinks into the horizon.
The green of the leaves
falls, brown, to the ground,
here to nourish the soil.
All shapes and sizes,
failures and success,
scars and celebrations.
Let them fall.
Let them be.
Free to decompose,
transform
into something new.
From the darkness
comes the light.
From the soil,
purpose.

If you've ever had your hands in deep loamy soil, you will never forget it.

The rich black color, soft without grit, earthy and moist without being damp, it just feels like fertility. The recognition that it can facilitate growth also comes with an innate optimism, a promise of life on which our very existence depends: what you plant, grows.

In many ways, the same thing can be said for generative community. And, once you truly experience it, you never forget it.

We feel connected, seen and supported, creative. Accepted, accountable, and inspired to take action. This kind of community is an invitation into the wondrous side of the collective human experience that anchors us in meaning and purpose.

With community as with soil, there's just something that you come to know, deep in your bones, something that we don't often have the language for. Outside of the realm of soil or social science, it's hard to quantify. But it touches on all senses, both grounding us and urging us forward. Thinking about relationships we create with others through a soil-based perspective, we recognize that sometimes we might not fully be able to understand or articulate the benefits of healthy conditions—but that doesn't mean you can't feel, sense, and know it when it's there.

It's like describing a great team you worked with: What made that possible, at that time and with those people? Why did you feel such a strong sense of connection and community? Nothing quite seems to capture the essence. But once you experience it, you spend the rest of your life seeking it out, working to recreate it. When those conditions are present, there's a transcendent quality, the capacity to generate the most remarkable things.

So it is with healthy soil.

If we trust that natural systems have something to tell us about sustainability and interrelatedness, then there is significant learning to be found when we think about leadership as a soil-building process. First exposed to this on Dr. Takekuma's farm, I have made it a throughline of my work in leadership training and development within institutional and community-based settings, with people from all over the world.

This co-creative process, from the start, decenters the *what you know* and invites in the *who you are* as an essential ingredient to both individual and collective learning. When these (and other) pieces are put into place at the right time, it creates the conditions for deeper realization and even transformation.

And it is the same when it comes to that deep loamy soil.

Very likely, that living soil is a result of many seasons of thoughtful stewardship, planning for things like cover cropping (planting crops for what they add to the soil with no intent of harvesting), compost amending (changing the nutritional composition of the soil by adding natural fertilizer), and allowing it to fully rest, outside of production. Such activities take time, space, and a keen attention to myriad relationships, not just to a short-term idea of immediate yield.

Such open-minded and open-ended work can be scary—it can feel like a risk—but it is what makes it possible for the most remarkable things to happen within that soil.

A HANDFUL OF SOIL

This can't be real.

That was my first thought as I stepped into the four-foot-deep trench that had been dug alongside a row of gobo (burdock), ready to be harvested.

The multisensory experience was unforgettable.

Thrusting my hand into the rounded mounds that flanked the trench, I felt an earth that was pillowy and soft, earthworms probing and digesting organic matter, billions of microorganisms metabolizing life beyond the view of the human eye, and a smell of . . . life. It was a handful like no other I had experienced: not an inert lump of earth, but a life force teeming with potential.

Looking back, it was at that moment that I began my trip from dirt to soil.

Even as I realized that this handful of earth contained so much learning, it was also profoundly humbling. There are quite literally billions of things happening in that handful that are beyond our comprehension and that one could spend several lifetimes trying to understand.

You can't know everything in that handful of soil . . .

It is a realization that has the potential to be diminishing or even paralyzing: If I can't understand this small fistful in my hand, how can I expect to understand this whole field? How can I possibly make decisions based on this incomplete information?

. . . yet a farmer still cultivates the field.

It is what happens after that first, overwhelming realization that is most important: successful farmers know to observe, listen, inquire, reflect, adapt, and adjust to what they learn from the ways in which their intentions and actions in cultivation meet the changing contexts in which they are planted.

I knew that I was developing an eye for farming when I started to see the field in a different way. The vibrancy of color and the subtleties of shape told me things that I didn't know how to interpret before I really learned to see their intricacies. Before I learned to hold the soil, these changes in the plants above ground would have sent me scrambling to find my information elsewhere: when to harvest, where to plant, how to water.

The first crop I ever planted independently filled me with dread, as I felt every ounce of responsibility for its success. Each seed, as it was drilled into the ground, was weighed down with the burden of responsibility that I felt, terrified by uncertainty and inflamed by my inexperience. But by the third or fourth planting, the experience had transformed: I was taking a trip with an old friend, the kind when you don't think twice if you're going in the right direction or whether you'll make it home safe.

One of the enduring myths of leadership is that some people are born leaders. But that's a notion of leadership that is driven by charisma. In fact, transformative leadership comes from doing the work required to develop fluency within your given context, whether it's a field in Japan, a boardroom in New York, a hospital in India, or a school in Uganda.

Whatever planting is for you—launching a new initiative, giving a public talk, teaching a class, or leading a team meeting—when you first do it, you don't have experience as you teeter from idea to practice. And until you build the muscle memory of experience, you feel the weakness of the connection between idea and application—whether it manifests itself in you as full-blown fear or nagging doubt. Real confidence is built by rooting down, not continually grasping, stretching, or projecting out through performance.

The journey from dirt to soil first requires you to put your hands into the soil and connect with it. That simple intent, followed by a commitment to exploration and inquiry, changes everything.

Connecting with the soil is about crossing a threshold, not arriving at a destination. This can make some people uncomfortable the first time they try. We are so deeply conditioned to think that leaders are obligated to fix, and fix as soon as possible, but putting your hands in the soil is about reaching for connection.

You reach into the soil because you want to get connected—bonded—to the field beyond what you can immediately see and touch. So where are we digging?

We are digging first into our own depths to see what each of us brings to the contexts in which we participate. A structured approach to building self-awareness, attention to your own context, helps us to see the world in a different way. A fundamental shift in perception is at the root of any significant transformation: the reconfiguration of our internal world of meaning as it rises up to meet the world around us anew.

Why do we dig? Putting your hands in the soil is not about extraction, it's about connection. It is about asking questions and staying, for as long as it takes, with the capital-W "Why" questions. It is not about checkboxing your way through the "whats" and the "hows" that occupy the lion's share of most leadership lists.

Connecting to the soil is about plugging into a deeper level of awareness and not losing sight that yes, it's about plants or it's about the things you do, but even more importantly, it is the context in which you do them and the care with which they are done.

ROTOTILLER WISDOM

The small tractor had just made its second pass over the ground where the green leaf lettuce was grown, and we were getting ready to rebed and prepare for a winter seeding of radishes. Dragging behind it was an old-model rototiller, its paint job well-worn and blades dull, but more than up to the job in the soft, loamy earth. Chopping and turning, it spun through the ground with little resistance, and in its wake was a fully brown-black soil that looked like nothing I had ever seen before. I thrust my hand into the ground, and then my forearm, ultimately reaching in up to my shoulder. Had I wanted to take the full plunge with my head, I could have done that as well.

This was the beginning of my second week on Dr. Takekuma's farm, and prior to that, I had considered the earth beneath my feet to be a solid mass, hard packed and firm. While I had intellectually absorbed his first lesson, that a sustainable farmer grows soil, it wasn't until this moment that I fully understood what that *looked and felt like*.

Growing soil was no longer an abstraction. I could feel (up to my shoulder) that it was an embodied, and practical, strategy for fostering life. It felt like that soil could do and grow just about anything. It felt more like a deep pool of water than a wide field of earth, and I can vividly remember the question that overtook me that morning as I watched with awe while the tractor slowly made its passes:

How did this soil become like *this?*

When I posed this question to Dr. Takekuma later in the day, he offered yet another answer that would stop me in my tracks.

It is because of time, space, and relationships.

I was expecting (if not wanting) something more tangible and specific—even something more seemingly scientific—like some miraculous seaweed only found off the coast of Okinawa or the bat guano from local caves—but space, time, and relationships?

I don't want to overly romanticize this moment. The conversation was competing with the whirring of the rototiller, and it was more shouting than contemplative. Furthermore, the clearing of this field was not for my personal learning, and it being early fall, there was more work than the shrinking daylight could accommodate. This was not the two of us sharing a pot of tea and exploring the deep philosophical underpinning of building healthy soil.

No.

This was effectively a tractor drive-by where I could take this learning and nurture understanding—but on my own time, as there were kabocha to harvest into wheelbarrows.

TIME + SPACE + RELATIONSHIPS

Dr. Takekuma's rototiller wisdom felt like a koan—a riddle, a puzzle. It was exceedingly simple, terribly abstract, and wholly impractical. It felt frustrating too. If I was going to eventually start and build my own farm, I needed to know actual techniques—what kinds of soil amendments to add and when, how to properly till and clear a field, whom I needed to involve for such activities—the important stuff!

At that time, as an aspiring farmer, I was certain that my path to success would be forged by an understanding of these skills and practices. I wanted a formula. He gave me one. But the variables were not what I expected. For this reason, from day one on the farm, I took copious notes. There is no doubt that I looked silly with my little notepad, stopping to scribble from time to time and then staring out onto the fields like I had captured the most important knowledge. Of course, all this place-specific recordkeeping would be helpful for a potential future farm in Kumamoto that I would never, ever operate, but that didn't stop me from thinking I was becoming a better farmer through the process.

By the time I found myself with the opportunity to steward a six-acre abandoned lot in Southern California through its organic certification process, I had tinkered with the variables such that I felt like I had cracked the code.

Time: knowing when to plant, thin, stake, prune, harvest, cover crop, and rest.

Space: leaving sufficient distance between plants, keeping competitors in their own corner of the garden, and marking off the paths where human feet were welcome and where they were forbidden.

Relationships: the dynamics between soil microorganisms and creatures, between species of companion plants, the ways in which plants attract insects, and the interplay between the plants you cultivate intentionally and the ones that volunteer a bit too eagerly.

Those insights felt sturdy enough to make me a satisfactory farmer, and I took not a little bit of pride as my soil grew a little bit loamier with each passing season.

In the same way that biological processes in the soil take ***time*** to break down organic matter so that it can contribute to long-term soil health, so, too, are the quality and depth of human relationships correlated to the amount of time put into forming them.

Life also needs ***space;*** for the living things in the soil to thrive, they cannot be packed too tightly (compaction). In farming, spaciousness is essential to encouraging everything from aerobic activity to root growth, and so it is in life, where people also need the space (and boundaries) to connect and grow. Furthermore, paying close attention to how that space is designed and "held" in service to generating life is of the utmost importance. In fact, in Dr. Takekuma's orbit, the farm and its community-based purpose invited people to connect to a different way of being, which was not calibrated to the frantic efficiency obsession of modern consumption, and to show up in a space that valued their participation in a more humane manner, which prioritized connection over transaction.

And living things of all kinds depend on ***relationships.*** There is more to be said about the *quality* of those relationships, but before getting there, I need to parse out what *kinds:*

1. With ourselves. This is the largely internal, often beneath-the-surface work of better understanding who we are and the ways that we are shaped and influenced by systems and structures. This is the work of growing self-awareness.
2. With others. These are interpersonal relationships, whether with colleagues, employees, supervisors, funders, partners, stakeholders, shareholders, or the communities we serve, transform, or with whom we may transact.
3. With our work. This requires turning toward the question of "Why do I feel how I feel, think how I think, and do what I do?" and to what extent those purposes are clear and relevant to one's life.

Dr. Takekuma's farm wasn't just a farm; it was the beating heart of a larger ecosystem that consisted of a wide-ranging network of community-based groups and associations. When he started the farm (twenty years prior to my visit), he enlisted the support of the mayor and other public officials as a way to ensure that the farm, and all that was connected to it, would be supported beyond just an economic consumer base. Each year, he would give hundreds of public talks to groups all over the region, speaking to how the traditional Japanese diet offered a pathway to better human and ecological health. Tens of thousands would visit the farm and its adjacent public health care facility as well as attend the seasonal festivals on the property. This was a shining example of community-based agriculture, but also an agriculturally based community, with the farm at the center.

In a literal sense, the loamy and fertile soil of that farm was a product of both tangible farming practices *and* the intangible spirit of relationships within a community.

Over time, I came to realize that it was not just relationships in the community that supported the farm but also the clear purpose that drove the entire enterprise: to grow health and well-being everywhere. But this was not some slogan that was slapped onto T-shirts and boldly stenciled across the walls; it was a deeply felt sense in everyone that I worked with. For some that purpose was best expressed through their relationship to the act of farming itself, while others forged that relationship through food preparation or providing medical care. It was a sense of plugging into a source, their source of inspiration and purpose—and being a conduit, enabling that energy to flow through them and into their work.

Together, we brought our diverse experiences, goals, passions, interests, and perspectives to produce this thriving ecosystem. Many members remained for decades as pillars. Others, like me, cycled in and out, transforming—and transformed by—the community. A dynamic so fluid yet always in equilibrium, you'd almost dare to call it metabolic.

It was not a formula, but the description of a living and iterative process.

Time + space + relationships.

So what happens when we make the time and space for relationships to ourselves, to others, and to our work? How does building soil improve and grow our leadership?

RELATIONSHIPS WITH OURSELVES

When we make the time and space to tend a closer relationship *to ourselves, we develop a greater self-awareness and learn to reflect with purpose and intent.*

To focus on time, space, and relationships can feel like a luxury—especially when it comes to our relationship with ourselves. Gravity and urgency pull us toward transactional over transformational connections. Even in a soil building approach to leadership in which you are prioritizing relationships, spaciousness, and time, the urgency of leading means that things come at you relentlessly. A never-ending treadmill. Spinning plates on stilts. As reaction elbows aside reflection, we are wired to crouch in the defensive. And without that strong connection to self, we can find ourselves quickly adrift, ungrounded, and disconnected from what fuels our purpose.

In my own work, when I find myself in this place, I am not at my best. I tend to be in a state of contraction, ask fewer questions, and, as a result, make poorer decisions. In some cases, I can feel myself closing off to outside stimuli as I try to protect myself from the overwhelm. The sheer number of decisions a leader is called upon to make, and the speed with which they are required to make them, can feel like a threat to survival, shutting you down and pushing others out. And never mind the challenge when working with others who are also feeling closed and defensive! The collective weight of a group of individuals all in a defensive posture can feel insurmountable. In that kind of compacted, fumigated soil, it is nearly impossible for expansion, creativity, or learning to take root.

So when we build soil in our organizations and relationships, it is critical to first focus on cultivating a generative, safe, and challenging space of learning and growth, including for ourselves. We are so often taught that the leader's job is to know the answer (sometimes even before anyone poses a question), emphasizing expertise and mastery over openness and inquiry, but knowledge and learning cannot be an either/or; they must be a both/and.

Soil building requires us all to do our best to hold an open heart and mind. In my work, I have learned that this is much easier said than done and that leaders—especially those who are leading social impact work—find it particularly challenging. Encouraging these leaders to take on a *beginner's mind* and become aware of how to work with each other from an *inquiry-based* mindset is a critical departure point from which new learnings and perspectives can be stacked upon.

You might think of this work as creating space within yourself.

Staying open means not seeking to "fix" others but rather cultivating your own capacity to work together with others to find clarity and resourcefulness through deep listening and open questions. Staying open means maintaining the space within yourself to honorably receive others' truth while ensuring no one gets to be wrong or right. It means working to reexamine and become more aware of your own beliefs and assumptions. Staying open means that we make mistakes and embrace the learning that comes from those times when our intentions misalign with outcomes.

In order to stay open, sometimes we need to pause. Running an organization can feel like a race against time, driven by fear of competitors or running out of money. Running a social-purpose organization can feel like a race against evil or injustice. But if that running turns only into running away, you will lose connection with our sense of purpose in small and, eventually, large ways that undermine our efforts and drain the nutrients from our soil.

We need to go at a slower pace than we've been taught—without fearing compromised productivity.

We need to take more and different spaces than we've learned how to occupy, to expand our aperture and let more settle into our field of view.

We need to change our cadence because the current one isn't working.

When we practice these things, we come into relationship with the soil and connect with our sense of purpose.

RELATIONSHIPS WITH OTHERS

When we make the time and space to tend a closer relationship to others, *we develop relationships that have greater alignment, whether we are serving someone, or transacting or transforming with them.*

When we give time and space to relationships, we do the hard, slow work of getting to know others and letting ourselves be known—not as full, complete beings baring our souls, but in a way that's fitting to the context, whether we are transacting, conversing, or cocreating (as I discuss in chapter 10).

In an output-worshiping world, slowing down in this way can feel like swimming upstream.

You may feel resistance to this very idea in your own body right now. But the growth that time, space, and relationships make possible is growth for the long haul. It is the key to the sustainability of your organization and of you as a leader.

Building on the foundation of our self-awareness (relationships with ourselves), we can come to these relationships more conscious of our own patterns, behaviors, privileges, and biases—and center an approach of discovery. And what results is something that every workplace and community knows is necessary: trust.

In many ways *trust* feels like the new *collaboration*: the thing that everyone agrees is vital to foster, but very few know how to create well. However, trust is even more precarious and delicate than collaboration, as it can take a long time to grow and but a moment to lose. Like a root system in the soil, trust grows outside of view and underneath the surface, drawing upon the nutrients of context to feed its growth.

There are few vocations that rely on trust more than farming. Even as modern agriculture prioritizes scientific predictability, still we must trust that the sun will lead to photosynthesis, the sky will bring moisture, and seeds we plant will sprout.

Even more so, the sustainable farmer trusts that natural life cycles will lead to their intended outcomes. In prioritizing the growth of healthy soil, the sustainable farmer works to cultivate the conditions outside of their field of vision, beneath the surface and in the realm of roots and microorganisms. They know full well that they'll never know it all.

But a farmer who has been through a full season on the land, observing which plants, pests, and weeds thrive, getting to know the density of the ground beneath their feet as it shifts with the weather and the seasons; a farmer who knows which beds need amendments, which need crops, and which need rest; a farmer who senses what lights up the faces of the people who come to market—that farmer is the one who has grown their awareness and is ready to take the right action, to the best of their ability.

Not the oblivious farmer who steps onto an empty field and starts throwing seeds in the ground, digging holes, or running irrigation lines on day one.

To someone deeply immersed in farming, this idea would be truly ridiculous.

Trust is not possible without building this awareness of what surrounds you and encouraging others to do the same. And then, through that collective act of inquiry and meaning making, a virtuous cycle of seeking and cocreating understanding together, we find that trust and connection with others is a natural output.

Yet if we translate the metaphor into the world of leadership, it might not land the same way. So much of our language about leadership prizes boldness, taking action, failing fast—sunk costs be damned—that we have no shortage of leaders who, indeed, rush to plant seeds in the very infancy of their tenure because they are taught that is what it means to be a leader. I'm talking about those with the best of intentions (I'm not interested here in those who show up and fumigate the entire place on the first day). I am talking about those who take their place at the head of the table, whatever its size, and apply the tools they've collected elsewhere in this brand-new context because they think that is what it means to be a leader.

Take the executive director who partners with a newly minted consultant to address an equitable workplace mandate in their first month on the job. They run a report on salaries, expose everyone's compensation to one another, and within a matter of weeks, the place is hemorrhaging employees. Why wouldn't trust and transparency grow here? It's not the values that are the problem; it's the soil.

RELATIONSHIPS WITH OUR WORK

When we make the time and space to tend a closer relationship to our work, *we can think and plan from a place of purpose and intent.*

When I say *work,* I am referring not just to compensated labor. I am pointing to the things that we create and build, the fire that drives us to act and ignites our sense of calling. Those things might be our families, our creative passions, our religion. They may have nothing whatsoever to do with the daily activity that pays the bills. Our compensated labor may be the source of our fire, and it might also be what douses our fire, causing us to burn out.

If you have ever built a fire, you know that what makes it burn is not so much the logs and kindling, but the spaces in between them: a breathing space where air can flow and provide fuel for the flames. So if those logs are piled on too tightly, it can have the same effect as a bucket of water, quelling the flame and reducing the fire. For this reason, fire building and fire tending require paying close attention to the spaces in between the logs; managed with great care, a fire can go on indefinitely.

So, too, is it often with our work.

Tasks or meetings or obligations or responsibilities, the "logs" pile up—and at an alarming rate. It is not about good or bad logs but simply the amount: in any case where there are too many and they are poorly configured, the core flame will reduce in size and scope. This is the same with someone who is overwhelmed, buried, or slammed: their core flame is at risk of diminishing or even burning out.

When that light is out, we have no flame of inspiration to share with others, no true leadership capacity. However, when the flame is strong, the act of igniting another fire only multiplies; it does not subtract. Fire has this remarkable replication effect; unlike other elements, it is not a zero sum when given away. Within leadership, it is vital that people tend to their fires and, more specifically, create the time and space necessary for them to grow and thrive.

COMPOST HAPPENS

I cannot end a chapter on soil building without reaching for the lowest-hanging—yet juiciest—fruit.

Compost.

Much of the work I did in the years after leaving the farm involved stepping away from the literal teachings and seeing what remained in the form of dirt underneath my nails—the lessons I carried with me through any number of spaces, many of which were bounded by four walls, a roof, and a floor. In my efforts to unearth the mystery of healthy soil, I always returned to the bread and butter of any sustainable farmer's soil-building agenda.

A dirty word for many, compost is finally having its day in the sun. There are composting initiatives, composting influencers, and composting products that promise to sanitize the practice within an inch of its microbial life.

But I'm not here to proselytize about the virtues of reducing food waste (although I certainly endorse it). I bring up compost for what it shows us about metabolism—the process that best captures my understanding of the kinds of transformation that result when we cultivate the conditions by privileging time, space, and relationships.

In my life and work, I often use this word to refer to how we can transform experience, memory, and nostalgia from its original (or imagined) state into something more useful to our lives as we move forward.

So often, we get stuck. Weighed down by our assumptions. Glued to our self-righteousness. Nailed to the ground by something we can't quite release.

Other times, we're charging full speed ahead, with no time to stop and ask for directions.

How do we transform something into energy? How do we make things *happen?* It's a question of balance.

To create good compost takes skill, discernment, and a sense of balance. Carbon and nitrogen, the accelerator and the brake, are a dynamic duo if ever there was one: too many leaves and food scraps invite "bad" bacteria to proliferate and result in a soggy, stinky mess or a pile that burns too hot, resulting in the dramatic outcome of firefang; too much straw (carbon) and the pile will take its own sweet time before turning into anything that resembles something other than what it has always been.

As a result, I was hypervigilant in how to manage that carbon-to-nitrogen ratio—I became a compostologist, and with my "compost happens" T-shirt, I was proud to be a part of this life-giving process.

Learning to tame this balance between carbon and nitrogen offered me one of the foundational lessons in soil building: action and reflection need to go hand in hand. In leadership, if we reflect at the expense of action, we won't make it through the workweek, and if we act without reflection, we may last longer than that, but we will leave untold wreckage in our wake

But probe the compost pile a bit deeper, and it's got yet another lesson to offer.

After some months of assiduously balancing my pile, I started to lose sight of what actually creates the conditions for transformation: the diversity of materials. Yes, it is a balance of straw and leaves, but also the *kinds* of straw and leaves that really help the most. The more varieties, the better the pile transforms into a mound of "black gold."

And here, too, the leadership lesson presents itself loud and clear: reflection and action are two modalities, but that distinction shouldn't overshadow the myriad things that make up each one. We best reflect when we gather as many diverse materials as possible, turning them over in every possible way, to inform the kind of action we should take (which sometimes means taking no action at all). And this is what both Inquiry (chapter 3) and Reflective Practice (chapter 4) will teach you, to gather the different kinds of materials available to you by building your capacity to look at situations from different perspectives and with different objectives.

A compost pile metabolizes best when we tend to both the balance *and* the diversity of materials it is being fed. Such attention does not in itself yield transformation and change (that is the role of the digesting bacteria living in the guts of the worms we coax into the pile). But it does catalyze a metabolic process, transforming a collection of somethings into a unifying thing: the Soil of Leadership, where anything you plant grows.

Soil Building and Leading in Nigeria

"I came to realize that the soil in which I had planted my organization and team members was not healthy. I used to want to know every detail of every project before it was executed, and I had very strong views about how each project should run. I realized that this stunted the growth of my team, and my team was unable to make decisions when I was not available. I made changes to my behavior and started thinking of what conditions I needed to create for the soil to be healthy again. I started to delegate more power their way, loosened my control quite a bit, and allowed my staff to shine (coaching and mentoring as they go). This has led to phenomenal growth both in individuals and on projects as people started blossoming and felt a sense of belonging and self-worth. Ideas started to flow, and rather than me saying "this is how we should do things," there are now a lot of great ideas, and I feel less stressed and even challenged.

But the biggest impact I experienced from shifting my perspective and focusing on soil building is the meaningful connections that I have cultivated and the love I share with my team. As a goal-oriented and result-oriented individual, I used to be laser focused on the result/goal and paid little or no attention to the people driving the goal. I was always focused on the plant and not on the soil. With the soil-building principles, I have grown to develop meaningful connections with people on my team, and I have seen how this has transformed my leadership exponentially. My team knows that I care about the results and our goals, but they also know that I care about them as individuals, and I am available to help them navigate challenges to achieving the goals and results. This has led to increased productivity and growth. I understand that growing good soil requires self-discipline as well as dedication, which often comes from continuous reflection and learning, so my work is not done, and I need to continuously work to nourish the soil."

Molade Adeniyi (Nigeria)
Chief Executive Officer
WAVE

The Language of Soil Building in Nepal

"I am deeply committed to creating meaningful spaces where women can freely share their stories. At The Story Kitchen (TSK), we believe that by honoring and preserving women's narratives, we can dismantle oppressive systems of gender and patriarchy. We strive to archive these stories, ensuring that future generations remember the profound contributions of our grandmothers and mothers. To cultivate an environment where women feel comfortable sharing, we focus on creating a safe and empowering space. Similar to nurturing soil for healthy growth, we bring awareness, understanding, and intentional language to build a supportive foundation. This deliberate soil building plays a pivotal role in allowing women to unburden their traumas and experience transformation through storytelling. The transformative power of storytelling is evident when I witness women sitting in our circles, sharing their experiences. Through the act of storytelling, they often find solace in unburdening their traumas, leaving them with a newfound lightness in their hearts and bodies. It may seem magical, but it is not a mere illusion. This profound effect is the result of the deliberate and purposeful cultivation of our soil—the deliberate construction of conditions that allow growth and transformation to take place.

It can feel magical—but it is not magic. It is the intentional building of soil and the conditions for transformation. By recognizing the significance of soil building and acknowledging the role it plays in creating a nurturing environment, we ensure that our organization remains committed to creating a platform where women can courageously share their stories. With each story shared, we take another step towards breaking down barriers, challenging societal norms, and fostering a more equitable and inclusive future."

Jaya Luintel (Nepal)
Executive Director
The Story Kitchen

REFLECTION

As you complete this chapter, I invite you to take a moment to pause and reflect on the following inquiries.

- Close your eyes and imagine thrusting your hand deep into your own soil. Envision yourself with a handful. Does it feel soft and alive or perhaps dry and inert? Dense and muddy? How does it smell? What do you think would best grow there? This is the first step in moving toward reflection and inquiry. Write down the adjectives that describe your soil.

- Undertake a compost analysis: How much of your time (and energy) is focused on action, how much on reflection? Do you think you have a good balance?
- For your organization or work, what timeframe constitutes a "full season on the land"? Is it a quarter? A season? A year? A decade or more? Now look back at that compost analysis. How much of your time and effort is devoted to action and reflection focused on the problems of today, this quarter, the season, the year, the next decade, or more? Are your actions and time allocations aligned with your sense of a full season or, even better, a multi-season cycle?

CHAPTER 3

Inquiry

So proud
to ask twice,
weed once.
But
is it really
a weed?

Everywhere I looked, there was more to see.

Soil was not dirt but a conduit and context for relationships. Insects were not pests but valued community members contributing to the greater cause. Carrots were not just snacks but—with a little patience—a source of flowers whose nectar served as a beacon to those helpful insects. Weeds were not a permanent feature on our to-do list but an indication of something going on beneath the surface.

Dr. Takekuma's explanation that time + space + relationships lead to healthy soil on a sustainable farm spurred my capacity to see and locate things on the farm—both contextually and relationally—to grow with each day. My observational skills sharpened, and I was able to see things I didn't know previously were there: the details, the complexity, the nuance. My aperture was broadening, such that I could see life in ever-greater relief.

As a part of this growing awareness came an acutely felt new orientation to time.

A sustainable farmer submits to the deep truth that, despite our best efforts to try to push the growth cycle, things will largely grow at their own pace. A conventional farmer will work to influence the timing a lot more, cutting out some of the variables that might influence that time by leaning on chemicals, plastic, or machinery. But any farmer working in a field is still subject to growing cycles.

In synchronicity with the unmistakable prominence of diurnal rhythms and with growing cycles to attend to, I started to feel that time on the farm took on a more fluid and richer cadence than I had previously experienced. Perhaps it was the combination of thinking into the near and distant future about how to sow life, together with the immediacy of completing a never-ending list of tasks before the daylight burned away, but something for me was cracked open and transformed.

A taste of seasonal time can have a profound effect.

One of the core capacities of the Soil of Leadership is to recognize—and commit to—a different orientation to time.

Despite our impulses, it is not the job of a leader to respond the instant we are faced with a decision, a situation, an email, a text. There may be people in your organization whose job it is to respond with immediacy in every instance. Responding quickly may even be one of your best skills (or coping mechanisms), but the leader's main job is to assess context and scan the whole field. Yes, sometimes we have to do that quickly, but if we don't take the time to do it with full attention in quieter periods, we won't be able to do it with alacrity and real awareness when we must move fast. When leaders make the time to figure out why and how we frame questions, problems, and ideas the way we do, we also can make the space to look at things from multiple perspectives; only then can we grasp the fullness of the context and situation—to assess not just the plants, but the soil.

Choosing a soil-based approach has many benefits. One is that it puts us in conversation with our deepest assumptions, our unconscious biases, and our blind spots. Often, leadership starts with a vision or inspiration, but over time, if we only focus on tending that singular vision, our sense of scale and time can narrow to a kind of tunnel vision, limiting the leader's ability to perceive shifting context. This rigidity can kill an organization. Regularly reaching back to the soil breathes life into your foundational capacities, amplifies your sense of empathy, and expands your ability to look for potential problems or opportunities.

And it starts with inquiry.

THE WEEDS OF INQUIRY

"Is that one good or bad?"

It was a Friday morning—any Friday morning—and I could reliably turn and see one of the volunteers at my farm crouched on the ground, arm outstretched, finger pointed, asking me for guidance.

Inspired by the life of Dr. Takekuma, I was now two years into managing my own sustainable farm. I had my own six-acre plot in Southern California, where I was farming annuals, mixed vegetables, and fruits, and distributing to local markets and community groups. I tried to cultivate conditions on my own farm to be similar to those of Dr. Takekuma's in Japan, by encouraging the neighboring community to connect to the land by putting their hands in the soil we were building. One such community-based initiative was a Friday drop-in that allowed volunteers to join in whatever activity was happening: harvesting for the weekend markets, planting, or light manual labor.

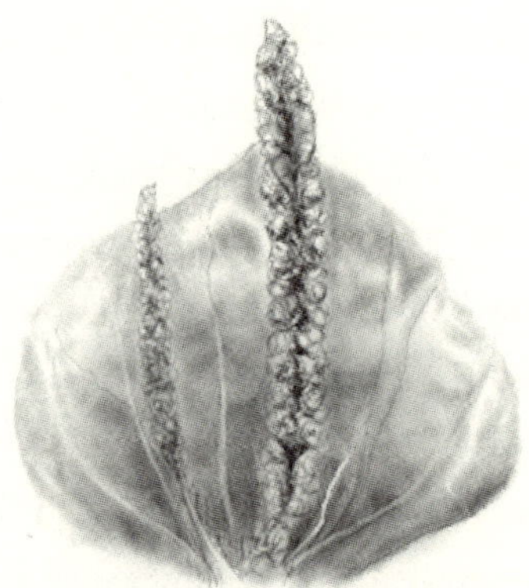

But as is the case on most sustainable farms, the ever-present task was to weed. While many preferred the exciting potential of dropping a new seedling into freshly prepped earth or grazing through a bed of strawberries while also filling up a full flat for the market, what we needed more than anything were people to help weed.

So it was common for people to arrive on Friday morning, be handed a tool and a set of instructions: "Those are pepper seedlings, that's basil, and that's parsley. You can pull out everything else."

It would be only a matter of time before I would hear my name being called and come to find them, crouched on the ground, arm outstretched, finger pointing, asking, "What about that one?"—undecided whether to pounce or to withdraw—"Is that one good or bad?"

Now depending on how my day was going, I had any number of different replies. On busy days, I might have shouted a quick "Pull it!" or "Leave it!" and let them get on with the task at hand. But if things were slower, that's when I'd explain that, in fact, no plant is good or bad, it all depends on the context. For our pepper-and-herb bed, anything outside of our three crops did not belong, because it wasn't one of the things we chose to grow there. It would take up resources we'd prefer to give to the plants we'd decided to cultivate.

But good or bad?

What if we ask a different question? It might take us longer to get a perfectly weeded bed, but I've found that when we shift away from judgment and into the realm of inquiry, everything has something to tell us—even the things that aren't "supposed" to be there.

Sometimes a weed isn't a weed but an open door to inquiry.

I submit for your consideration one of the most present plants on my farm: the broadleaf plantain.

Not a particularly attractive plant, the broadleaf plantain has oval-shaped, mottled leaves that lack the organization to resemble any discernible, collective form, and the flowering spikes tend toward pragmatism over beauty. Often found in distressed soils, the greens of its leaves suggest that it has better things to do than attract the human eye, and it seems like it is generally frosted with dust and other indicators of neglect.

Unrelated to its more valuable namesake (the plantain), the broadleaf plantain produces up to 20,000 seeds from each bitter-tasting plant, which quickly becomes tough and fibrous in its life cycle, thus making it low on the food-choice ladder for herbivores. Which is unfortunate, because the plant can quickly grow in just about any nook, cranny, or patch of earth and, just as fast, overtake tender seedlings.

A weed if there ever was one. A weed that you don't need to be a grizzled farmer to know is not supposed to be there.

Pull it and move on.

Or do we?

Could the unconscious reaction to a deeply held assumption be glossing over some deeply held truth? What if we take a moment to surface and parse it? Could my understanding be getting in the way of generating new perspectives and inspiring creativity? How can I be so sure that something is the way I believe it to be?

It is said that the broadleaf plantain made its way to the Americas on the ships of the Puritan colonizers and, therefore, came to be known among some Native communities by the name "white man's footprint." This is due to how the plant thrives in disturbed and damaged ecosystems, and at that time, it was very present in the areas surrounding European settlements. Far from the most pernicious or damaging of colonial exports, nevertheless, the ubiquitous presence of the plant throughout the North American continent is a reminder of that "footprint."

But apart from its adjacency to the arc of colonialism, the broadleaf plantain is a messenger. It grows most frequently in compacted soil. Which is to say that, when it is growing somewhere, it is telling us something: this soil, and the conditions under the surface, may need help.

It is an easy plant for our farm volunteers to identify and evaluate. But to eagerly dispose of it without inquiring into its presence and indications is to overlook important information about that soil, that context for growth. Pull the plantain now, but that won't be the end of the story. In that plot of earth where broadleaf plantains proudly plant their flag, those peppers may have poor odds of surviving, let alone thriving.

Good plant or bad?

The broadleaf plantain makes an apt emblem for inquiry because it is a reminder of how the quick formation of judgment closes off possibility and other ways of knowing. Inquiry is about finding the broadleaf plantains in our life that we are certain lack utility or benefit—the things we want to rid ourselves of as quickly as possible—and revisiting them with new eyes and a curious, open heart.

In leadership and management, your broadleaf plantain may be the team member who has been labeled as a "troublemaker" or "problem" or the fixed explanations of why there are struggles within certain business collaborations. Like with weeding, through assumptions and repetition, things quickly become sorted into "good" or "bad," and the opportunity to revisit those (often) snap judgments gets lost in the busyness of work.

When we stay longer in that place of inquiry, suspending judgment, if even for a brief time, we discover new ways to see the things around us and what they may be telling us. It is what helps us to get under the surface of what we can see and closer to the roots of how we know. And learning does not require us to go outside of our experience, but rather to turn toward the familiar assumptions, patterns, routines, and behaviors and wonder why.

A DIFFERENT KIND OF INQUIRY

We all ask questions.

A leader is told to ask good questions, hard questions, to challenge and inspire their team to go the extra mile, achieve that audacious goal.

Asking questions is part of the job description.

In a world where leaders are valued for their performance, the questions we are taught to ask are impact-based: What is the right solution? How will we achieve it?

With our eye on the prize, the preparatory steps are precious few. We sprint from intent (determine the problem) to impact (achieve the goal) without coming up for air, leaving no time or space to consider the assumptions informing that very straight path nor the very alternatives to action.

And yet, in between our intent and our impact, there is an opportunity for learning (and growing in self-awareness, as we will cover in chapter 9). A space that we can open up that breathes oxygen into our compacted soil. Instead of pulling the broadleaf plantain and tossing it into the compost heap, we can recognize that those plants may have shown up because they have something to say: the soil is compacted here, and it needs time and space for remediation and restoration.

When we commit to the conscious and deliberate process of connecting to the soil on which we blithely tread—yes, at first, it might feel awkwardly slow—we begin to shift our orientation to time and space. Our aperture opens, so that we can see more deeply within ourselves, down into the roots of our assumptions and beliefs, and connect more deeply to others, understanding more of their story while recognizing there will always be something beyond our understanding.

This connected-soil approach drives a different kind of inquiry.

Inquiry is not just asking questions.

In his seminal book on transformational education, *Pedagogy of the Oppressed*, Paolo Freire writes that without inquiry, "individuals cannot be truly human." He continues, "Knowledge emerges only through invention and reinvention, through the restless, impatient, continuing, hopeful inquiry human beings pursue in the world, with the world, and with each other." In this way, inquiry is not simply a space for problem-solving or a way to find convergence; rather, it sits at the very heart of how humans come to individually and collectively make meaning in the world.

For those working in fields or sectors aiming to shift perceptions (and I would argue that there is an element to this in just about every field and sector), inquiry is the pathway to create change and build new and/or deeper connections. When we stay in inquiry, we stay in the realm of possibility and discovery. This is especially the case when our impulses toward judgment (and all that can come with it) can be tempered, suspended, or extinguished (in the next chapter on Reflective Practice, I will introduce a foundational tool for how to do this).

Inquiry lives at the very heart of the Soil of Leadership, and it is not only a state of being but an open passage to discovery that all leaders need to be able to access if they wish to cultivate a deeper connection to themselves, to others, and to their work. And while circumstances often dictate that we cannot remain in a place of inquiry and curiosity for too long of a time, it is the rush to react and judge that inherently closes off possibility.

An inquiry-based approach to leadership helps to slow down reactivity, tempering that impulse of leadership to just take action and create impact. It shifts the focus away from the urgency of what you know to discernment of what you do not know. And, in much the same way that Dr. Takekuma's simple but fundamental conventional-sustainable farming distinction, discussed in chapter 1, opens distinctly different pathways, an inquiry-based approach challenges leaders to open themselves to new perspectives and look differently at the world that has become so familiar.

So often in our work, in our leadership, or even just more generally in our lives, we are living in the world of reaction. Things are happening around us, and we are largely unconsciously responding. That response is, in a very, very simplified way, the result of our experience over time of how we interact with the world. Our impulse is simply to pull the weed.

FLOATING ROCKS

If I hold a small rock in my hand, and I drop it, and someone tells me that it falls to the ground every time because something called gravity exists, it's confirmed every subsequent time that I take that rock and drop it. Children love to drop things on the floor, just to see what will happen. Gravity is new to them. As an adult, I don't question gravity; I am generally not even inclined to explore it. This is because every time I have tested gravity, my expectation has been confirmed. That alignment of what I expect is going to happen and what actually happens gets filed away into the unconscious as a truth. This kind of evolution is good. We don't want to be questioning gravity every time we pick up our foot.

As we move through the world, our experiences go from being fresh to familiar. Where once we puzzled things out, now we turn on autopilot.

Now, if I were to take that same rock and drop it, and it did not fall to the ground but floated up into the air, that unexpected event would cause me to question the very foundation of my beliefs. Inquiring "What is going on here?" I move from that unconscious, reactive place to one that is more reflective, in order to move toward a place of new discovery, so that I can have greater clarity about whatever it is that is leading this rock to not fall to the ground but float to the sky.

So much of our time in our work and our life in leading is taken up with responding to all the things that are around us. In a world that evaluates leaders and leadership based on outcomes, sometimes asking divergent questions can feel indulgent, or even irresponsible. Leaders are constantly pushed to make decisions without the time to reflect on the information that might be contained within a given experience or incident. We often feel there isn't time or space to consider how best to respond, let alone to contemplate deeper questions of why the organization or group is doing something at all or how it got into this situation in the first place.

How do we enter into and stay in inquiry? How do you slow things down so that you can collect more information about what's going on, so that you can make better decisions?

It starts by changing the kinds of questions you ask.

An impact-based approach privileges what and how and "right" solutions, whereas the inquiry-based approach prioritizes asking: Why?

Pushing toward the "why" of things creates new spaces for reflection and discovery, as well as for creativity and forward motion. Asking the right questions and being open to exploration is what enables us to get under the surface, into the soil, and get at the roots of things.

The moments in leadership that push one toward inquiry are rarely as startling as a floating rock. But next time you see something that just doesn't make immediate sense, resist the urge to drag the rock back down to earth. Maybe it's floating because it's not a rock but a helium balloon. Maybe it's floating because you're on another planet, which means you're either dreaming or an astronaut. Either way, before you figure out how to approach this unidentified floating object, you're going to want to get curious.

GROWING PICKLES

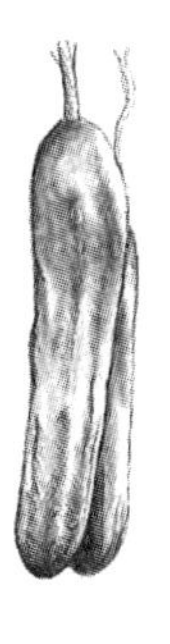

"When will there be pickles?"

It was an honest and unguarded question from a dear friend.

We were halfway through my farm tour, which I had been honing since my return from Japan, over repeated visits from friends, relatives, and willing acquaintances. With each visit, I felt like I had taken a step closer to integrating the pieces of myself that I had fostered in various settings since graduating college.

Grateful for their willingness to step into my new world and eager to develop a pedagogy that would connect any nonfarm-inclined person to the power of natural systems, I took it upon myself to engage all their senses, especially taste and smell. And, on this particular walk, my friend had been softened by the sweetness of heirloom strawberries and the kick of fresh chiles. Sensations rare, yet familiar, dialing back his intellect and opening his heart.

We were walking the perimeter of the farm, and I was expounding on why and where certain things were planted; not for their capacity to produce food for humans, but to attract certain insects, like the braconid wasps that were likely to prey on pests like cabbage worms. And as I pointed out a row of dill—an umbellifer plant, whose ample nectar and small florets make it easy for the fast-moving braconid to fuel up—he asked the question "When will there be pickles?"

"Oh," I said off-handedly, in what I hoped would have been a quick parenthesis in my presentation, "We don't process food on the farm. As I was saying . . ."

"No," he said, not taking my cue to keep walking but instead gesturing toward the dill, "When will there be pickles?"

It took a moment before I understood, and in that instant, it was all I could do to hold respectful body language. Juggling between shock and judgment, I caught my balance when I saw his face: pure curiosity.

He honestly believed that dill plants produce dill cucumbers, or as they are commonly known, dill pickles. He wanted to know when we could expect to harvest the briny, sweet-sour delicacy and enjoy its crunch in the field, much like I had invited him to try with the chiles and strawberries moments before.

I have thought about this moment many times since it happened, two decades ago.

Not because of how I eventually responded (I explained how and where cucumbers are made into dill pickles), but more for what it taught me about how our perception is limited by our position and how "truth" comes to be constructed.

For my friend, the relationship between dill and cucumber was defined by his experience of opening a jar. That is the context for his understanding. In this respect, the question was wholly rational. In his world there is no cucumber plant. The origin story of the crop is outside of his view.

Until he asked me that question, I took it for granted that everyone knew where pickles came from. To be honest, I never even considered that might be something someone *didn't* know. But by asking myself *why* he thought that, I got two things.

First, I got insight into my own assumptions about how people relate to the food they consume and what it means to try to engage them around that relationship—which, at that stage of my career, was one of the primary things I was hoping to achieve on the farm. If I was going to help foster connections to the natural world, my pedagogical approach was going to need some fine-tuning. The fountain of knowledge—which to me had felt like a generous pouring forth of all the wisdom I had earned by the sweat of my brow—was not the model that resonated with my actual purpose. I can't say I left this interaction with my teacher-self transformed 180 degrees, but I had gained some distance from the way I had been unconsciously showing up.

Second, I got the opportunity to come closer to my friend, to foster rather than compromise our connection. I left the door open for him to share more about why he thought that, to be vulnerable and reflect on his relationship to food and to nature. I found myself being more connected to him because I experienced an authentic moment of vulnerability, where he was expressing, unintentionally, a lack of knowledge, something that I knew how to fill, but I didn't respond in a way that would lead him to close himself off.

Let's take the pickles back into the workplace. Conversations like the one I just described—they happen all the time. Two people are looking at the same plant; one sees beneficial insect food and the other sees pickles. Both are truths, incomplete yet incontrovertible, their validity confirmed only through additional context.

In your workplace, do people feel comfortable asking "When will there be pickles?" Do you feel comfortable asking question for yourself? Are there assumptions that prevent you from understanding how someone could *not* know all the things you know?

STAYING IN INQUIRY

When we make the time to stay in inquiry, we're more likely to leave the space and time for our relationships to develop and to sideline the kinds of impulses, like shame and condescension, that diminish and silence honesty and often come from a place of fear. There is a correlation between generative inquiry and psychological safety. When we feel comfortable and safe to the point that we can pose open and honest questions, a spirit of discovery and connection can grow. When we feel insecure because our questions are likely to be met with the force of superiority, only the most hardened weeds can sprout. We can also call the former healthy soil, where the conditions have been cultivated for transformation, whereas the latter will require all kinds of external inputs and superficialities for anything to grow.

Maybe at the end of the day, after we've given space to ask ourselves and one another "Why?" we haven't converged around a single answer: dill plants are both food for beneficial insects and the prelude to a pickle. But inquiry allows us to accept divergence. You may not come to a point of clarity, but there may be new ways of understanding things.

And that's what leaders need to be able to do: converge around points of action while allowing for divergent perspectives to coexist.

If the leader is afraid of inquiry and what it might disrupt and/or unsettle, then others will not be comfortable to step in and participate in the kind of work that generates deeper connections. But this is an all-inclusive point, as even the most open-minded and open-hearted leaders struggle when they feel the basic premises of their work are being questioned. Yet this is when it is most important to sit in inquiry, even when that inquiry feels like fire.

Holding that space, before we follow the seemingly gravitational pull of our convictions, is harder than it seems. The longer we stay in a space, the better we think we know it—until we stop thinking about it at all, as it moves from new to familiar. When you sense that you don't know anything, it is easier to be open to everything. So, too, is the converse: when you think you know everything—or at least tilt toward that—you tend to be more closed than anything.

Staying in inquiry takes practice.

It also is not a place we can stay forever.

In fact, there are plenty of times where we want to be decisive, clear, and not open to myriad options. Leaders do also need to move with conviction, but there is a balance to be struck. Take, for example, the medical emergency that demands immediate action, where life and death hang in the balance. There's no time for questions, only action. But the reality is that most of us (hopefully) are not faced on a regular basis with the kinds of significant events that demand immediate action. Yet we typically respond to phenomena in our lives as if most everything demanded the same level of reactivity and immediacy.

So the key to staying in inquiry is to slow things down and shift from being reactive to being more reflective, bending and reshaping our relationship to time so that it better serves our leadership and decision-making. And because time is a core ingredient in the process of soil building, it is vital that we have the tools to slow it down.

And how is this done? This brings us to the theory and application of Reflective Practice.

Inquiry and Reshaping Perspectives in Uganda

"As a leader in the work of girls' education and women's empowerment, an inquiry-based approach is essential in everything I do. I often encourage my team members to question traditional notions of leadership by asking: "What qualities make a great leader?" and "How can we challenge gender biases in our definitions?" Through open dialogue and collaborative learning, I have been able to create an environment where my staff and the community members we work with can explore new perspectives, challenge norms, and contribute to reshaping the narrative around gender. Staying in inquiry is something that I try to practice often at work. When I make the time to stay in inquiry, I am able to create a safe and inclusive environment where honest questions can be posed and diverse perspectives can coexist. This fosters psychological safety and allows for deeper connections to form. This is essential because I also engage and work with vulnerable women and children. I have been able to challenge my own assumptions and encourage others to do the same, paving the way for growth and understanding. It requires me to be open-minded, even when my fundamental beliefs are questioned, and to engage in uncomfortable conversations."

Monica Nyiraguhabwa (Uganda)
Founder and Executive Director
Girl Up Initiative Uganda

Staying in Inquiry in Peru

"Among other things, staying in inquiry enhances creativity in the classroom. Instead of simply implementing standardized teaching methods, we asked ourselves what can we gain if we looked at the importance of creativity and the role it can play in education. This led us to recognize that fostering creativity encourages critical thinking, problem-solving skills, and a love for learning. With this insight, we explored innovative teaching methodologies and incorporated arts and crafts, storytelling, and project-based learning into the curriculum. An inquiry-based approach has enabled us to challenge the traditional notions of education in Peru and opened up new avenues for exploration and growth. Most importantly, we see remarkable transformations in our students' engagement and enthusiasm for learning: they are more active participants, expressing their ideas and developing unique solutions."

Yessica Flores (Peru)
Cofounder and Executive Director
KANTAYA

REFLECTION

As you complete this chapter, I invite you to take a moment to pause and reflect on the following inquiries.

- When was the last time someone in your organization asked about "growing pickles"—asked a question that may have seemed outlandish or naive but revealed something fundamental about their (or your) understanding of your organization's work or purpose? How did you respond?
- Do you want your organization to be a place where people feel comfortable asking questions driven by pure curiosity and feel comfortable admitting they do not understand what is going on?
- If so, what are three ideas you have right now that might encourage that kind of open inquiry in your organization? Are there ways you already know you can change your own behavior to encourage people to ask questions about growing pickles?
- If you don't know how to encourage that kind of open inquiry in your organization, you can set it as a team goal. Ask others to propose their ideas. If your organization is hierarchical, you can even do something as old fashioned as setting up a suggestion box for people to provide anonymous ideas.

- Do you have good indicators of issues beneath the surface in your organization? Who (or what) are the broadleaf plantains in your organization? Look back on some of those who have not succeeded within your organization: What can their failures and successes tell you about the state of your organization's soil?

CHAPTER 4

Reflective Practice

Reflection
on action
is to know
the fruits.
Reflection
for action
is at
the roots.

After about three months on Dr. Takekuma's farm, firmly in the early stages of my steep learning curve, I was becoming more connected to the experience and the place. I was now doing a much better job of stepping in the right places, cutting at the right angles, and thinning at the right spacing. The clarity and simplicity of my work, combined with the importance of precision, made each day feel purposeful and made me feel a part of something bigger than myself.

My relationship with the soil on this farm was real, my actions shaped by if and how they were positively contributing to its health.

And it hit me: I had fallen in love.

I was smitten with learning through all of my senses, by how the work of my mind and body could inform each other to create fertile ground and delicious produce, by the ways in which body and mind—when aligned—could create a more exuberantly alive result than either in isolation. I was enlivened, from deep within my heart, by the alignment of purpose, community, and objectives.

I was fully awakened and connected to the power of soil building.

I was head over heels for the way we harvested the fruits of past intent and sowed the seeds for a hopeful future, all in the same hour.

I adored the way that people's faces lit up when they took home the produce and delighted when they returned for more.

It was a whole-body quality of connection, grounded in that local earth and animated by the supportive community. And each day, as I was opening myself more fully, my self-confidence and comfort grew. I was proud to be asking fewer how-to questions and to be better able to properly interpret gestures from my Japanese-speaking colleagues.

With each small win, my curiosity was giving way to conviction. Far fewer were the disorienting dilemmas that defined my start, and I was happy for that. I felt fully arrived, welcomed into a community, and more whole than I can ever remember.

Love was in the air.

But as can be the case, I was becoming blissfully unaware of how my heightened emotional state was narrowing my perspective on discovery. For while love was wonderful, I would soon learn that this emotional state was not a destination, but that it lived most dynamically when equally fed by a clear intent to stay open and listen deeply.

THE LANGUAGE OF DAIKON

One of the most unmistakable learning edges in human development is when we find ourselves in contexts where we lack the language skills to seamlessly experience everyday life. When we lack words—as anyone who has been directed to a bathroom in a language they don't understand knows—we look to other forms of communication, like physical gestures, to fill in the gaps. Unquestionably underresourced, we attempt to make meaning of others' words and actions, becoming comical in our assumptions.

At the same time, we are hardwired to seek understanding. As our familiarity with cultures, words, and gestures starts to grow, so, too, does the drive toward clarity of meaning. In more simple terms: When it comes to language, the more *I think* I understand, the more assumptions I make about what I am hearing. And when I'm in this mode, my interpretations tend to be way off.

This was certainly the case for me while living on the farm in Japan, having arrived there with little to no language capacity in Japanese. It is all too Asian for me to say that I still experience some shame and embarrassment at this fact, though I would end up learning how to speak and even read and write Japanese. And yet until I came to Japan, I had wanted very little to do with the language. The extent of my familiarity came from the experience of being around my *nisei* (second generation) grandparents, who spoke English at home but would liberally use an older form of Japanese to curse and talk about food (and of course to have conversations that they did not want me to understand).

As a result, I arrived on the farm with a crude Japanese that equipped me to dine impolitely in a mid-twentieth-century sushi restaurant, and little else.

Yet, as is the case with immersive experiences, after several weeks of living in a monolingual (Japanese) environment, my language skills (and confidence) grew significantly, alongside my comfort in the field. The love of the farm made me bolder, more willing to throw myself into conversations, even if I knew odds were good that I wouldn't last past sentence two. Make no mistake, this was growth from the grunts of a two-year-old to the monosyllabic speech of a three-year-old. Still, I was proud, and slowly but surely, I started to allow for more assumptions about the world.

And it was at that point that I was given a gentle, but enduring, lesson.

After three months, despite my powerful feelings toward the farm experience, I was still a novice. Appropriate to my capacities, I was assigned basic things, like harvesting, weeding, and turning the compost piles.

During the workday, I was well supported by my coworkers—a few of whom spoke English. However, I was the only one living in the massive farmhouse, and occasionally members of the public would come by before open hours, putting me face-to-face with someone who needed something that required an elaborate game of charades to decipher.

A few mornings a week, the farm hosted a public market, and one day, as I was doing my premarket prep, I heard a knock at the barn door. When I slid it open, I saw an older woman I did not recognize. Probably in her eighties, she was stooped over but remarkably fit, like she could deadlift her body weight many times over.

After a quick greeting, she launched into Japanese, not stopping until I repeatedly gestured to her that I didn't understand. A look in her eye showed she registered, "Okay, this Japanese-looking fellow is really dense and cannot fully understand what it is I'm saying."

By then we'd moved into the foyer area, where there was already some produce that had been prepared the day before. She pointed at a daikon radish—a white, thick, long, icicle-looking vegetable that is one of the more prominent vegetables in the Japanese diet—and then pointed at the field.

I was able to figure out, "Okay, she wants a daikon." So I went into the field, found a classic looking daikon—straight, long, and round—pulled it up, and brought it back.

She shook her head and then pointed again at the radish. I thought, "Okay, maybe this one was not big enough or good enough," so I tried to gesture, "Bigger?" She did something else with her hands, which I interpreted to mean, "Go back and try again," so I went back and harvested another one. When I brought it back, this one was not to her liking either.

Thirty minutes in, I was frustrated—and impatient to get back to my responsibilities for that morning's market.

So I went back again and tried one more time—again, failure. At this point she looked frustrated as well, because here was this guy who couldn't understand but who looked like he should understand what she was trying to ask for.

Deadlocked with me in this "agree to disagree" place, she looked a bit resigned to take the radish that I had harvested. Then she handed over one hundred yen—about one US dollar—and left.

Very soon thereafter, people started arriving for the market, and I busied myself picking more daikon radish, carrots, lettuce, and greens, while my coworkers showed up—one of whom spoke English.

After the morning sales were complete, I mentioned to him, "This elderly woman came by, and I think I really frustrated her because I wasn't picking the perfect daikon for her."

My coworker said to me, "Oh, that's Suzuki-san (Mrs. Suzuki). She doesn't come by very often, but every year she comes by to honor her husband's passing—probably about five years or so since that happened. And she does that by gathering different things that were of significance to their relationship. One of the things is a daikon from our farm, and she has a particular feeling about how it should look."

As I listened to his words, the whole event replayed itself like a film, unwinding my interpretation of the difficult consumer refusing to abandon her never-ending quest for the world's most aesthetically pleasing radish, and reconfiguring it into a heartbroken widow honoring her relationship with her deceased spouse.

I had, over the course of my interactions with her, gotten entrenched in my sense of righteousness that I was doing what she wanted, when, in fact, I had no basis for that assumption, because I couldn't communicate with her. Beyond the words, I had no way of accessing the deeper purpose, but I felt confident that I did, because I had this idea that I knew what Japanese consumers wanted.

I also had an idea of what I thought the nature of the transaction was: people would come, and they wanted to buy a vegetable. But I didn't take into account that perhaps there may have been something on the other side that wasn't just about the consumer-producer dynamic: a depth of meaning buried underneath the thick layers of my half-baked interpretations. As I would come to learn, plenty of the visitors to the farm had a deeper purpose to their visits: the cancer survivor whose treatment was supported by vegetables grown in thriving soil; the families who used the outing to the farm as a temporary respite from their daily obligations.

But at that stage, even though I knew *I* had a deeper purpose on that farm, I saw our visitors as consumers. This not only limited how

I could interpret them; it also meant that for all my head-over-heels sense of openness, I was markedly limiting how I could relate to them, as I confined our relationship to the narrowest of frames: I had opened my heart to myself, but, in truth, my connection to others was superficial at best. I felt as if I was there to hand them radishes and collect their yen—the *work* component that justified the *study* on the other side of the hyphen.

If my colleague had not offered me a reframe, I would have missed an opportunity to connect to this woman's life and her experience. To not only understand, but to feel: How something that meant nothing to me was of great significance to her. How that gap presented a chance to form a greater sense of compassion and empathy for her loss. How I can connect with that feeling myself.

Like that daikon, the real gift that experiences have to offer lies beneath the surface, outside of immediate sight. And to access that gift requires time and space—two of our key ingredients in soil building—which I have learned can be effectively done by accessing a familiar tool: reflection.

REFLECTION

We are born to reflect.

To consider and reconsider things that happen in our lives is not only something that we all do; it is quite literally a distinguishing feature of our humanity.

And yet, while this might be natural, it is typically employed in an unconscious and unstructured manner that can distort rather than clarify. In the context of leadership, reflection has long been assigned to the realm of "soft" skills and thus discounted, underappreciated, and underexamined as a tool for both strategy and innovation.

But to be able to reflect on our actions, for the purpose of shaping our actions, is a critical capacity for any form of leadership that seeks to create greater connection. If the core challenge of leadership is to understand, to the best of our abilities, "What is going on here?" so that we can take the best, right action, reflection can help us to increase self-awareness, understand our impact on others, grow empathy, and develop new strategies.

Effective and connective leadership depends on Reflective Practice.

If we think about inquiry as a broad approach and mindset, Reflective Practice is a more specific tool and practice, one that is internally and relationally focused.

Reflective Practice is intentional, strategic, and purposeful. Leadership practices are very much about acquiring or honing the necessary tools to do things—a forward movement. Reflecting in a structured, intentional way is not very common, particularly in the realm of leadership.

Reflective Practice requires taking multiple steps back to begin to identify the unconscious and conscious beliefs, assumptions, and patterns that underlie our thoughts, feelings, and behaviors. We focus on questions like: Why might I think this way? Why might I behave this way? Why might others have thought or behaved this way?

And for all that we benefit from individual reflection and its capacity to reveal unseen aspects of our lives, when we integrate perspectives other than our own into the meaning-making process—like the compost pile that metabolizes into the richest soil, thanks to the diversity of inputs—we reach the level of understanding that best primes us to take right action.

The Reflective Practice framework is deeply informed by a social-constructionist perspective. In simple terms, it tells us that "reality"—our beliefs, actions, and interpretations—is shaped by social norms and interactions and not by some innate, objective truth. Reality is subjective, with layers of meaning that are the way they are because we agree (consent) at both an individual and collective level.

Yet at the same time, as macrosystems intersect with our individual identities and experiences, we often find that we are completely at odds with someone else's interpretation of an event. What one person intends as a joke, the other interprets as an act of disrespect. What is offered as solidarity can be received as condescension. Rather than intractably dig down into opposing camps or gloss over problematic encounters, Reflective Practice allows us to think about how these wires get crossed and what we can learn from that.

THE REFLECTION TREE

I find it helpful to explore Reflective Practice through a model. This representation of a tree and its roots speaks to how we both consciously and unconsciously make meaning and knowledge in our lives. Let's take a look.

Reflective Practice Cycle

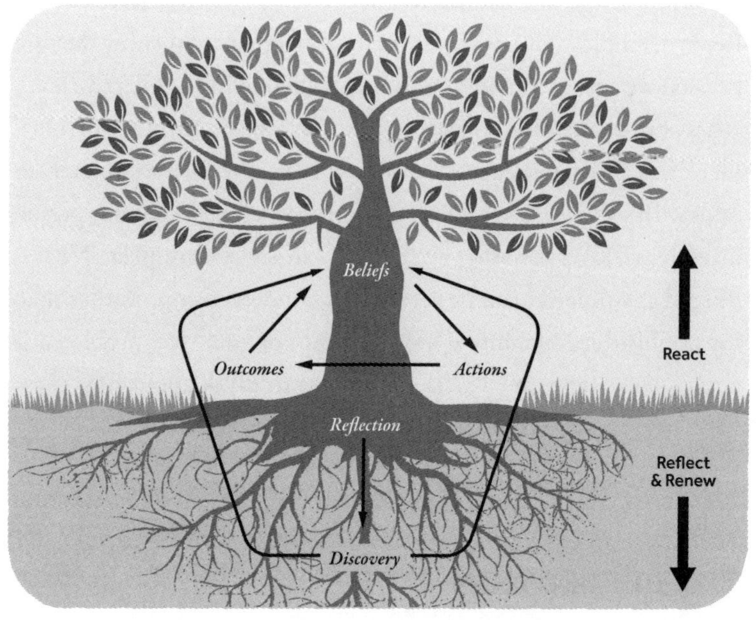

Starting at the surface, if we look at these beliefs, actions, and outcomes, this is what we might call the superficial nature of "the way and why we do what we do." But in fact, those things are informed, propped up, and fed by what's going on beneath the surface—the context, the soil, in both the individual and the system(s) they participate in. And to see and explore those things, we need to act intentionally, with a deeper sense of reflection and discovery. And so those are the roots. That's what lies beneath.

Using the Reflective Practice framework on my experience with Mrs. Suzuki, I can see that my feelings of shame about the gap between my Japanese appearance and my rudimentary Japanese language skills added a level of reactivity to my responses, shoring up my belief about the superficial values of Japanese consumers. My newfound pride at my farming identity also might have amped up my indignation: I knew perfectly well how to harvest a daikon; who was she to look down her nose at my *three* perfect selections?

I was fortunate that my colleague shed light on the experience with Mrs. Suzuki, bringing me one step toward understanding the significance of the encounter. But most experiences don't go that way; we rarely have a translator who reveals the missing piece of the puzzle to allow everything to make perfect sense. And even if we did, the point of Reflective Practice is not to organize around a singular truth of an event. The translator could give me some context that allowed me to dislodge my reading of Mrs. Suzuki as a persnickety customer, but only Reflective Practice could help me unpack how my own beliefs about myself were impacting the identities I was working on cultivating. It is something I engage with (at times wrestling, at times collaborating) to this day.

Ultimately, Reflective Practice helps us stay in inquiry and explore and discover new perspectives, and it can help develop a greater sense of compassion and empathy. We often think we should naturally be able to live into and easily practice our beliefs or always accurately feel into what other people may have been thinking or feeling in a particular circumstance, but it takes practice, lifelong practice.

THE FOUNDATION OF TRANSFORMATION

Reflective Practice is a tool to shift our relationship to time and space. It's reflection on action for action.

Imagine your organization is holding an event. You've been planning for months, and on the morning of the event, you arrive at the venue, only to find that your event planner had not secured the location. You're an hour away from the start time, with dozens of attendees about to arrive. You're pacing back and forth in the parking lot, sending text messages and making phone calls, one after another, scrambling between figuring out what to do to make sure the event doesn't crumble before your eyes and chomping at the bit for the planner to pick up their phone, so you can let off some of the steam that's starting to puff out of your ears.

"I'm so sorry," the planner says, when you finally get hold of them, "I thought we had an understanding with the venue. They've never asked for a formal agreement before."

In that ambivalent moment when your attention is pulled between dealing with this management mess and getting your event back on track, Reflective Practice offers a structure through which we can slow down experience and begin to understand the phenomena in our lives in more nuanced and deeper ways, disrupting our push to form meaning and judgment around our interactions with the world. Centering inquiry slows down the flow of assumptions by asking questions: What just happened? Why are things this way? Who has contributed to these outcomes? Is this how we want to be? Are there other ways of looking at this? What am I missing?

It encourages us to take emotional space from these phenomena and to use these new perspectives to inform our approach to work and life. With that space, we can turn ourselves back toward our own lives to get closer to the roots of our contributions to events. It offers a chance to "dig where we stand" and excavate new meaning and perspectives from past experiences, and to point that learning in a direction that enhances and grows our awareness.

This is the very foundation of transformation and change.

Here's how it works.

Facts

First, we begin with **Facts**—describe the event in as objective a language as possible: What happened? Don't get into how you felt just yet, and if you start to get pulled into the realm of emotion, just notice that and turn back toward description. That might well be the first lesson, when you recognize you struggle to describe the event without your blood pressure rising. It might look something like this:

> **Description:** We were supposed to hold an event at a local venue that we had used many times before. Planning had been in motion for over a month, and I believed that we had all the pieces in place to ensure a successful convening. When I arrived at the location, I discovered that, in fact, the venue had not been secured by our staff member in charge. At that time, the event was scheduled to begin in an hour, and we were expecting thirty to forty people. Furthermore, the staff member in charge was not at the location and had sent a message saying that they would be arriving late. They did not respond to texts and phone calls.

Emotions

Second, we enter the realm of **Emotions**, first yours and then others: How did you feel? How did others feel? Why do you think you felt that way? Why do you think they felt that way?

> **My feelings and assumptions:** We planned this event, and our staff didn't do their job. I was very surprised and upset, because I had assumed that this person would secure the venue. When I

tried to contact them and they didn't answer, that made me even more angry, and I was ready to fire them on the spot.

Others' feelings and assumptions: Since this was a venue that we had used before, maybe our staff in charge assumed that their verbal request was enough to secure the reservation and not have to sign a formal agreement with the venue. They felt comfortable that the location was set and there was nothing to be concerned about.

Analysis

Third, once you've laid out the facts and the emotions, you move to **Analysis**: What factors shaped this event, beyond the interpersonal dynamics? Were there significant power differentials? Did societal norms or constructions like gender, race, or class contribute to the outcome? This is where Reflective Practice starts to reveal and point toward discovery; the more you can dig, the better. (We will go deeper into the role of power in collaborations in chapter 4.)

Power and influence: The day before, I had asked if everything was set for the event. They responded saying everything was fine. Perhaps, because I am their director, they wanted me not to worry; perhaps they did not want to bring attention to themselves. My assumption that they would tell me if they needed anything was misguided.

Discovery

These three steps come together in the final step, **Discovery**. This is where we work to deepen our sense of empathy, trying our best to understand the situation from the other's perspective, really situating yourself there. How did what happened impact me? How did what happened impact others? Are there other ways of looking at this event that I had not previously considered?

> **Other ways of looking at this:** This staff member has been under a lot of stress lately. Their whole family got COVID. This person's father passed away recently, and ever since then they aren't meeting the performance level that they used to. Missing such an important thing, like confirming a venue for an event, is not like them, so maybe they are struggling in ways that I have not been sensitive to. They have been working with us for over five years, and I do trust them.
>
> Is it possible that it was not the staff member's fault—nor any one individual's—but a systemic problem that speaks more to the ongoing issues in our organization about communication? Have there been other instances like this but in other contexts?
>
> Perhaps, even though we have worked together for a while, I have been particularly edgy lately, so they were afraid to tell me they hadn't secured the venue?
>
> Could it be that someone at the venue dropped the ball?

The outcome of Reflective Practice is to better understand the various angles that may inform the outcomes of situations so that you, in your leadership, can make better decisions and take the right action for that context and moment. It is *not* to give a free pass to others. What action you choose to take will vary with your purpose as a leader, your relationship with the others, and your team dynamics.

You may decide the event planner's lack of communication with you about their difficulties is a sign of a broken rapport that jeopardizes the organization's cohesion, or you may decide you need to explore different forms of support to help them get back up to their past performance levels. You may even start to uncover patterns as you repeat this practice in the context of multiple events: maybe it's not just one employee who has a hard time trusting you; maybe it's widespread. Maybe what happened is more on you than anyone else.

So now the time you've spent on your Reflective Practice starts to pay dividends, as it points you toward the next right step. Whatever answers you come to, you might require further work, further assistance, further exploration.

Reflective Practice isn't an endpoint. It's about slowing things down, so we cultivate the conditions, rather than leading with our fists clenched. Which means we must always ask: what is our purpose?

In this case, was my goal to be able to successfully put on events with zero margin for error? Yes. So if I think the event planner is incapable of contributing to that goal, maybe I need to let them go. But if by reactively firing them, the output is that I terrorize the others on my team, or if I am setting others up to take the fall due to the poor culture of accountability I have created, I probably haven't taken the time to properly reflect and learn what I really need to learn.

Each of the steps of Reflective Practice provides a piece to a larger, unknowable totality of a puzzle of "What's going on here?" These are just ways of being able to fill in things that are not immediately visible: you need some prompts, you need a structure, you need some things to help you to get to the roots. There's no one magic answer.

It's a bit like looking at a tree that isn't producing fruit in the way you expect. If you only attend to the leaves, you're missing a large part of what makes up the totality of that tree—the root structure and what it's planted in. But you're not going to be able to dig up those roots and look at them straight on without killing the plant. You've got to learn to perceive and interpret the things that are right in front of you that have never caught your attention or have long since faded from sight.

Sometimes, the chance to see something in a different way comes from thinking about why someone doesn't really speak your language when, by all readily apparent measures, it seems that they do.

As Reflective Practice shifts and reshapes our relationship to how and why things happen in our lives, it broadens our scope of vision to better answer the question "What is going on here?" so that we can, as leaders, take more informed action.

It is also an important way that we, as leaders, can do "the work."

Before we can have any real conversation about things like equity, diversity, trust, and collaboration, we need to understand what's going on, not only *around*, but also *inside* you. If you celebrate the terms and skip the work, you hollow them out—like the farmers' market vendors who scoop up produce from a wholesaler, put on some overalls, and call themselves sustainable farmers—ultimately creating a gap between rhetoric and reality, where cynicism proliferates, and fundamental change goes to die.

Cultivating *your* conditions, your soil, through Reflective Practice is how you grow the things that thrive and grow in *your* context. They're unique, not uniform or consistent with how they show up in other places. And like with sustainable farming, that's part of the beauty—the unique, bespoke nature of the things that thrive in the soil of your leadership.

There is a saying, "We lead from who we are." But in the context of the Soil of Leadership we might say "We lead from who we are and where we are rooted." Or, even better, "Our fruits are only as strong as our roots."

Reflective Practice helps us discover a greater connection to both roots *and* fruits—the very essence of who we are and where we are rooted.

Power of Reflection in USA

"In the world of marketing, I've discovered the game-changing power of reflection. As a storyteller, taking the time to look back and analyze our experiences with partners and beneficiaries has been eye-opening. It's like digging deep into the outcomes of our marketing initiatives and campaigns, finding what truly strikes a chord with our target audience, and figuring out what works and what needs improvement. By reflecting on our past actions, I can fine-tune my approach, make smarter decisions, and keep moving forward. Reflection isn't just about the numbers and outcomes. It's about understanding people on a deeper level. When I reflect on how our marketing efforts impact our beneficiaries, it helps me get inside their heads and better meet their needs. It's all about building genuine connections and empathy. In the fast-paced, high-tech world of marketing, people might overlook reflection as a low-impact activity, but to me it's a catalyst for driving innovation and forging meaningful connections.

Embracing reflective practice lets me constantly improve my marketing strategies, adapt to changing needs, and bring real value to our organization and the people we serve."

Gia Riney (USA)
Chief Marketing Officer
Diocese of Nashville

Reflective Practice in Nepal

"I am determined to play my part in the most burning issue of today's world, climate change, through the conservation of biocultural diversity. But sometimes I find myself anxious and frustrated either with myself or other people and stakeholders that I interact with. Though I was taking different personal and professional courses, I would always fall back to my own old pattern and was not able to change what I envisioned. This is when I was introduced to Reflective Practice. Reflective practice enabled me to dive deeper into myself to be an observer of my own actions and analyze different perspectives by recognizing my preexisting assumptions and judgments. This also enabled me to be open-minded and develop critical thinking to understand various perspectives from others' points of view. Getting into the habit of doing intentional and purposeful reflection has fundamentally shifted how I think and act. Reflective practices rejuvenated myself from inside out, created a whole new version of me who is resilient and would be able to carry the sustainable transformation."

Kushal Poudel (Nepal)
Cofounder and Director
Avni Center of Sustainability

REFLECTION

As you complete this chapter, I invite you to take a moment to pause and reflect on the following inquiries.

- Do you have a daikon story? Consider a time when you were stuck in a loop of miscommunication with a coworker, employee, friend, or family member. Apply reflective practice to that experience of disconnection.
- Did you bring assumptions to your daikon experience? As you look back at these assumptions, how do you feel? Do you feel, as I did, some sense of shame or regret? If so, what do those feelings tell you about your assumptions and whether they are aligned with who and how you want to be?
- How could you have turned that incident into a catalyst for reflection? Think about where in the miscommunication loop you could have taken the time to reflect. Try to dig down and identify the elements of context that you could not see then.
- How would you have shifted your perspective and actions if you had been able to take a pause and identify the roots of that miscommunication at that time?

CHAPTER 5

Fallow

Something's wrong
when here
in the dead of winter
I long for offseason.
Yet the soil
keeps producing.
Be in awe,
delight in the
unexpected blooms.
Abundance
thrives
in a
tended fire,
and evaporates
under the
weight of
too many logs.
A pause in the arc of infinity
does not stop time
but honors it.
Fear not the time of fallow.

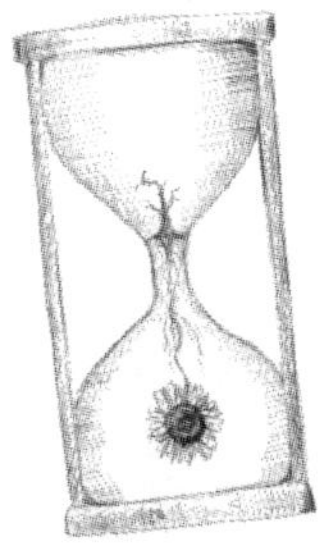

"There's not enough time in the day. I need more time. Can there be thirty hours in the day instead?"

It was a playful, rhetorical question posed to me in a one-on-one coaching session with a leader from East Africa. The charismatic founder and executive director of a successful community-based social enterprise, she is recognized globally for her work and leadership with women and girls. With hundreds of staff members and tens of thousands positively impacted by the work of the organization, the demands on her time and energy are significant. And this is without taking into consideration her domestic unit, with three children under the age of twelve and a large extended family. It is beyond question that she knows what it means to work hard, prioritize action, and maximize her time.

It was a surprise to her when I replied to her query with a question myself: If you did, would that be a positive thing for you?

She paused, closed her eyes, drew in a long breath, and with her exhale, let out a deep sigh.

"You know, I know how to produce and perform, and I know that I am good at it. I get energy from setting a vision and doing whatever is necessary to achieve it. I love inspiring people to action, and I take pride in being the person that people turn to for help. But the truth is, I don't know how to rest. And there are no good role models around me, as everyone else is in go-go-go mode all the time as well. The other day I took a 'vacation' with my family, and I spent most of the time on my phone or laptop, tending to work issues that only I could fix. And if I'm being honest, I like that feeling of responsibility; it gives me purpose . . . but I'm also getting more and more tired, and the work is just increasing as we grow. I just realized that I don't know how to rest, and I worry that inability is going to be the end of me."

Over the past twenty years, I have heard a version of this leader's reply countless times. We have learned to work and produce, but we struggle to rest and restore.

Why is this the case?

REST IS A FOUR-LETTER WORD

Like other four-letter words that are pushed to the margins of acceptable language, rest has weirdly found itself adjacent to ideas like weakness, indolence, and complacency. Perhaps this is no surprise for a production-oriented culture that celebrates "the grind" and "getting the most out of life" and embraces a consumerism that celebrates outcomes and achievement.

The world over, we are all encouraged to work hard, lean in, live large, and treat every moment as if it were our last. Those who do are celebrated and held up as role models who are "making it count." If we are to believe the mythology, to pursue anything less suggests you are falling short of your potential. Whether it is a student who studies late into the night, the entrepreneur who spends weekends shaping their business ideas, or the community leader who functions on three hours of sleep to be available to the people they serve, these are faces on the posters and memes that get passed around to inspire others to the same. There was an American athlete who branded himself with the saying "no time to sleep" as if to indicate that there were too many things to do and not enough time to do them.

So it is not only that in our production-oriented economies there is never enough time to do what you need to do, there is also a culture that supports and celebrates the "doing" aspect of our lives.

I encourage you to question and even reject this frame.

I reject it because of my many challenging and life-draining experiences as an entrepreneur. I reject it not because I am tired, but because people (never mind leaders) cannot be at their best without rest.

Rest is the fuel of the wise.

While the drive to push past perceived boundaries is a premise worth considering (i.e., making your life count), when pursued through a production mindset, the process is shaped by choices that favor extraction over restoration and doing over being.

The unspoken truth is this: like the leader in the story that opened this chapter, people the world over are questioning their own capacity to continue doing the work they are doing, at the pace they are doing it. And as I increasingly work with younger leaders, I see and hear that this is not an issue that is confined to a certain age or level of experience; we are all being pushed to live and lead on a razor's edge, to push until we can push no more. Because of the ways that hard work and "the grind" are celebrated and because of the public facing, performative nature of positional leadership, which requires a projection of confidence and strength, leaders do not have the spaces to express what I believe to be an existential threat to creating a better world.

The hard truth is that too many are scraping by, moving from emergency to emergency. Many are running on empty.

And if they cannot continue to do the work, then we will not be able to address the social and environmental crises of our time, build and grow new businesses, and more generally advance innovation in the world.

It is people—not things—who advance the work, and without people—without leaders—everything will fall short of its potential.

And despite what the dominant economic narratives might have us believe, these people—you—are not so easily replaceable.

Making space is not a failure; it is a strategy for longevity and sustainable work.

I am not speaking against hard work, making your life count, or even "grind culture." It is not the idea or the mindset itself that is problematic. The problem is that we too often think it is the whole picture—the whole field of view is taken up with the grind—but it is just a fragment of what should be understood in a larger whole. And it is this narrow, segmented approach that is the problem.

It is another cause of narrowed vision.

The difference between growing plants and growing soil illustrates the importance of opening your field of vision.

DEPLETED NUTRIENTS

The growing-plants, production mindset that drives so much of the "doing" approach to life and to leadership often has a single-season focus and emphasis on doing whatever it takes to increase that season's yield. But since this is not sustainable, external inputs are typically required to accelerate or override natural processes, and the adrenaline of immediacy shapes action.

Over time, repeated extraction depletes whatever nutrients may have been present in the earth to the point of scarcity, and dependencies rise as the cycle of production accelerates and compresses to meet the demands of precarious consumption: plant, manage, harvest, and repeat.

Growing soil, on the other hand, situates production in a larger context, understanding that there should be no extraction without restoration. We push and challenge the ground to provide, but never lose sight of the truth that healthy plants thrive in healthy soil. It is, therefore, vital that we build that soil to be as healthy as it can be.

If the farmer is focused only on maximizing this season's yield, they will sacrifice the long-term possibilities for production. So, too, with the leader who focuses so intently on this quarter's results.

There are now a handful of books that encourage us all to rest, but I want us to look specifically at how you can integrate it into your leadership. One of the core tenets of the Soil of Leadership is how we shift our relationship to time and space.

This is the practice of fallow.

Heroes and Martyrs

Before moving forward, I would like to pause and offer a brief reflection that may or may not resonate with your experience.

Over the years, leaders of all kinds of organizations and businesses have asked me these questions:

- If you don't give of yourself fully, how do you know you are doing enough?
- How do you know if you are working enough, if it doesn't hurt or feel like sacrifice?
- How can I justify taking a break when others are at the office doing their work?

These questions come from a genuine and heartfelt place. They are not self-aggrandizing; they are self-sacrificing. But often self-sacrificing and self-aggrandizing are not so far apart.

If you have built a project, organization, or business that cannot survive without you, for which you are the center of the universe or the singular lynchpin, then even if you are sacrificing yourself to help others, you have an outsized perception of your own importance.

It is true that there are rare leaders whose presence is essential to the cause, but those leaders are mostly the stuff of myth.

No one, in my view, is uniquely and solely strong and capable.

That doesn't mean your leadership isn't important, even critical, but that also doesn't mean that you are the only hero who could do the work, and it certainly doesn't mean you are the only martyr who can catalyze the movement. If you are trying to put yourself in that position, then that is your choice, but do it with intention and clarity about your (perhaps overblown) sense of purpose.

I am not talking here about being the only breadwinner in your family or the key member of your community. I am talking about your perception that if you take just fifteen minutes of rest, the whole world around you will crumble.

Is this you?

THE IMPORTANCE OF FALLOW

In agriculture, fallow is when a field is left unsown for an extended period of time for the purpose of restoring fertility or to allow it to rest from the churn of production.

We tend to assume that any farmer would prefer that their field(s) be in a state of production, but farmers focused on the long term learn to value the fallow.

I can remember on my farm in California how the mere thought of taking a piece of land out of the production cycle created a knot in my stomach. How could we make up for the lost potential revenue? This was something I could not afford to do.

But on the farm, what a soil-based approach taught me was that it was precisely the opposite: *not* letting the land rest was something that would eventually lead to degenerative outcomes.

So I planned for periods of time—some months, some full seasons—when select plots of land were taken out of the rotation for planting. Not only to give it rest, but also to allow for the kind of restoration that would be necessary for it to be producing at its best.

At first it was hard to see a bare piece of land as a positive thing—especially when I knew that under a plant-based approach I could account for any deficiencies in the soil with the application of external inputs, like chemical fertilizers. Allowing for "nothing to happen" on that plot felt counterintuitive to a production mentality that wanted a process that turned over every piece of open ground to the outcome of food production.

Then I realized that the way in which I was making meaning of fallow—how I was interpreting it—was shaping and distorting my farming practice. I was seeing it as an act of "nonproduction," where nothing was happening, because I was so focused on the idea that activity and productivity were tightly correlated.

And upon reflection, it was no surprise that I had so much resistance to putting my fields in a state of fallow.

I felt that being in a period of fallow meant that not only was I not producing, but also that I was falling behind. This sense of being surpassed, the internalized norm of industrialization and capitalism, can fuel heightened anxiety. In this mindset, a decision whether or not to choose fallow is weighed down by a judgmental—almost combative—frame: are you on or are you off?

And it is this active/inactive binary that is so problematic and degenerative.

I thought I had to learn to trust that what appeared on the surface to be "nothingness" would eventually lead to greater production.

In fact, I had to learn that fallow *is* production.

Fallow is a state of restoration and renewal.

And restoration is rebuilding. Renewal is rebirth. To be rebuilt and reborn is power.

Without fallow, soil cannot grow.

In some ways, we can say that to choose fallow is to act radically, to actively claim a space and the time for restoration and renewal in contrast to an industrialized system fueled by extraction and exploitation. But restoration and renewal should not be radical acts. They are essential components of leadership.

What I learned about fallow from my time as a sustainable farmer and as an organizational leader is that fallow is about a *connection to time* that prioritizes restoration, wholeness, and rest. It is not an on-off switch.

It is not the opposition to production and action, but an essential element of what makes it possible for any of us to act and produce at all. That may seem to be a matter of semantics, but the difference is real and significant.

We cannot have production without restoration and rest.

We cannot build sustainability into our systems—whether they are sustainable farming systems or human organizational systems—without structured and deliberate restoration and, as we discussed in the previous chapters, reflection. These practices are multifaceted and take time, but it is not simply time "away" from work—it is the time in true rest that makes action possible.

I know some executives who seem to grit their teeth and endure vacation (for the sake of their families, for example), or who plan every bit of time "off" to the minute to maximize it, or who cannot reflect or rest without alcohol or other inducements.

I am not saying there is anything wrong with planning an action-packed vacation for your family, filling every minute of your time away from your desk with activities, or enjoying a good mezcal. I am saying those things are not the same as rest(oration). Take a minute and ask your body whether they are the same. Your body knows the answer.

I am also not saying there is anything wrong with structure.

Fallow does not mean drift. In fact, fallow requires intention. And in order to set that intention effectively, you must learn to truly and deeply value fallow and the role it can play in your life.

INTENT, TIME, AND SPACE

So then, what does fallow look and feel like for those who are not sustainable farmers?

For me, my periods of fallow are characterized by these three qualities: intent, time, and space.

Intent

This is one of the things that sets fallow apart from simply "unplugging." Intent means that the act of stepping back and away from a production mindset comes from a place of purpose and intentionality. There is a *why* associated with the action. Fallow—the practice of rest and restoration—is important for the long-term sustainability and success of any leader. But its power lies in how it is connected to purpose. When you rest and renew yourself, what more are you capable of? Perhaps it is being more creative, inspirational, and motivated. Perhaps it is so that you can be more present for the people in your life. I know for me, my fallow time is directly connected to my overall well-being and emotional and mental health. Whatever it is for you, it is vital that you get clear on the what and why.

Time

The time horizon in a period of fallow is intentionally periodic. On a farm it is seasonal or annual, but this is not to say that, like a farm field, you need multiple months to restore (although you might, and that is okay), but rather that fallow time should be regularized. It could be about taking fifteen-minute, purposeful, and intentional breaks during the course of a busy day or assigning one day every week for no busyness. I regularly block off fallow time in my schedule, especially after activities that require a lot of my attention and energy. I make sure that I have significant, uninterrupted stretches of time (days not hours) where I can be more focused on *being* rather than *doing*.

Space

For fallow to be effective you need to "take space" from the ongoing flow of your life's patterns. Whether this takes the form of emotional and/or physical space, it is an important act of disconnection from action, which in turn creates more room in your mind and heart for building connections with people and ideas when you complete your fallow and move back into the realm of "above the surface" action. It involves setting boundaries and, when coupled with intent and time, it means asserting your presence and agency. It took me a long time to learn (and accept) that taking space—*my* space—was not an act of weakness or failure. I am speaking to the importance of what it means to know your needs and tend to them. Or, put differently, to understand your soil and how to best steward its journey toward well-being.

If you find yourself fighting the fallow, think about where and when ideas and inspiration come to you. Is it while you are multitasking, frantic, during a day of back-to-back meetings or while you are scrambling to get dinner ready or kids to school? Or do those solutions and innovations come to you in the shower, on a walk, bike ride, or jog, after meditation, during the calmest hours of the morning, or after everyone else goes to bed? If you find yourself in this second list, then you have had a taste of the benefits of fallow.

Creating Fallow Time in East Africa

"Being a medical doctor often means that I have to take care of others all of the time. This leaves very little time for me. I have, therefore, learned to take deliberate steps to create Fallow Time where I do reflections. To me this is often on Sundays where I have decided not to do any clinical work but focus on myself and my family. Throughout the week I take a few minutes to have quiet time and reflect on the plans of the day as well as the lessons that nature offered me from the previous day. By the end of the week, I have enough information to reflect upon and realize where I can change. I review these and refine my responses in future circumstances when presented with the opportunity once again. My work is not without challenges, so I have to practice self-reflection before I respond to some of these challenges."

Dr. Robert Kalyesubula (Uganda)
President and Founder
ACCESS Uganda

Rest and Restoration in Bhutan

"Rest and incorporating the practice of fallow has made a subtle, but significant, impact on my life. In the demanding field of academia, where constant productivity is often valued above all else, I have come to recognize that rest is not only essential for my own well-being but also for the quality of my work and the growth of my students. I have allocated specific time for fallow periods, where I dedicate time for my Well-Being Practice. By giving myself permission to pause, I am able to replenish my energy, gain new insights, and foster a greater sense of creativity. By embracing and valuing rest and fallow periods, I have seen the positive impact it has on my own well-being and the quality of my work. Resting allows for restoration, renewed perspective, and enhanced productivity. It is through these intentional breaks that I am able to cultivate a healthier and more sustainable approach to leadership, one that values the long-term growth and success of both myself and those I work with."

Kuenzang Dolma (Bhutan)
Law Lecturer
Jigme Singye Wangchuck School of Law

REFLECTION

As you complete this chapter, I invite you to take a moment to pause and reflect on the following inquiries.

- Look at your calendar and carve out a time for fallow—try to plan it out a full quarter, or even a year. Then ask yourself how it feels.
- How does it feel to envision yourself with time for fallow in your life? Is it freeing? Energizing? Intimidating? Fear Inducing?
- If you imagine your life with time for fallow, what is your first impulse? Is it to grow your organization or self to take up all that space with new initiatives, projects, people, or programs?
- Now, envision yourself or your organization in three, five, or ten years, having incorporated time for fallow. What might be possible as the result of your prioritization of rest and restoration?

CHAPTER 6

Spaciousness

The fullness of life
is only possible
thanks to
the emptiness,
the spaciousness,
the unmeasurable
openings
in the soil
that invite
the roots
to explore their potential.
Deep growth
made possible
not from what
is,
but from what
is not.
Set your roots.
Tend your earth.
But remember,
it is absence
that makes their presence
possible.

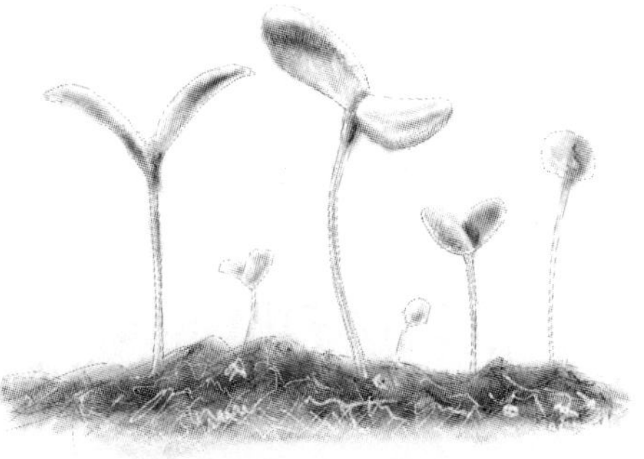

On a sustainable farm, space matters.

To ensure that myriad relationships thrive, a farmer must mind the spaces in between: newly planted seeds and seedlings, fresh furrows and rows, layers of organic waste on the compost pile, even between microorganisms in the soil. Above ground, not enough space chokes off full potential; too much compromises production goals. Below the surface, the success of root systems and the very survival of microorganisms relies upon thoughtful spacing.

Of the soil building trinity introduced in chapter 2 (time + space + relationships), space—and by extension, spaciousness—has surfaced as a dominant theme in my life.

In school, I was drawn to the field of geography for its diversity of thought and its critical acknowledgment and reckoning with its disciplinary roots in colonialism and imperialism; I was trained to understand space as an organizing principle with/through which to look at the world. If time is the purview of historians, space is the geographer's domain: we concern ourselves with how it is represented and experienced as both a lived and imagined form. If nothing else, geographers are all about space.

On the farm, I learned to see, measure, and appreciate space. In academia, I learned to examine space for its invisible power dynamics, its unexpected relationships, its impact on lived experience that often evades notice.

But in organizational leadership and community life, I found a chronic lack of awareness of (let alone appreciation for) space and spaciousness. Our cultural obsession with scaling new heights, covering more ground, climbing ladders, smashing ceilings, and being productive leaves us with a single spatial axis: onward and upward. Our talk about space is largely about capture, consumption, and climbing. We are only interested in space insofar as we are passing through or filling it, even devouring it.

What if our relationship to space were fundamentally different?

Not as a container to be filled or exploited, but as a key to context. A fine-tuned awareness of space that pays attention to relationships between things and how those relationships shape outcomes is a key tool of insightful, generative leadership. What if we paused the locomotion and inquired into the air we breathe, the ground we tread? What if we made it part of the leader's task to make and comprehend space, taking into consideration not only how much space we occupy (seeking to "right size" to take up more or less of it), but also how we relate to it and to the ways we let it (and ourselves) be?

SOIL COMPACTION

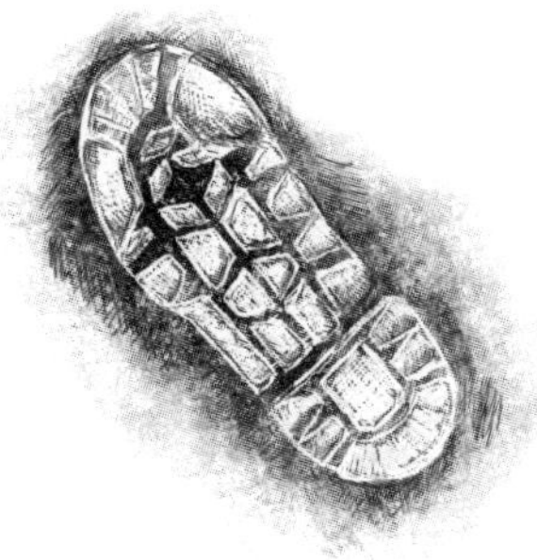

Early on in my farming life, I developed an obsessive concern with people's feet and where they landed in the fields. As much as any pest or plant pathogen, human footfall would be the ultimate destroyer of sustainability; a misplaced heel, slamming down on freshly tilled earth with as much pressure per square inch as a heavy track grader, leads to an outcome I was so furiously focused on preventing.

Soil compaction.

The process of cultivating a healthy, thriving soil—to encourage the ideal tilth—is predicated on healthy, aerated earth. One that facilitates an optimal exchange of water and oxygen within the spaces in between soil particles and plant roots. With good soil tilth, plants thrive, and the world beneath the surface teems with life and billions of biological interactions. But without it, in a state of soil compaction, life expansion is stunted, and diversity has no foundation in which to flourish.

So in the same way that a fire grows because of air flow and the spaces in between the logs, soil thrives in a similar, simple configuration: spaciousness that enables the flow of energy and resource exchange.

When you have it, life can flow and continue on indefinitely.

When you don't, life slows, and conditions become less and less hospitable for growth.

Soil compaction is no small thing. And once I learned that large farm implements, due to their intentionally designed weight distributions, are in many ways *less* of a threat than the simple human foot, it was all over. When people would step on planted beds, I could almost hear the collective screams of billions of microorganisms in the soil crying out in agony.

So we created well-defined pathways and scolded those who stepped outside of them. Visitors typically responded with an incredulous furrowing of the brow, but all I could sense were the billions of microscopic displacements happening under the heel of an unconscious fool.

It was all very dramatic.

But what I didn't know at the time was just how important a lesson

I was learning about leadership and life: space and spaciousness catalyze growth.

And it is in tending to the spaces in between things, whether it be from a perspective of time, place, activity, or responsibility, that we create sustainability. When a soil is compacted, very few roots can find their way in it, and as a result, growth and expansion are stunted.

Life needs space in order to thrive. And in our leadership, we can learn a lot from this truth.

CHOOSE SPACE

It was early April, and the soil was just a few weeks awakened from its winter slumber. While I had loved being on Dr. Takekuma's farm during the slowness of winter, I was ready for the spring and all the promise of a new year. A field had been prepared for a new crop of apple trees, and this was to be my first experience putting commercial trees into the ground. Unlike the visioning and anticipation that accompanies the seeding of a forty-day-to-harvest crop of lettuce, planting a tree, especially an entire acre of trees, requires a different kind of imagination—one that calls upon you to envision that what looks more like a branch, fragile and thin, might eventually grow into a large, thriving tree. But in this bareroot whip exists great potential, the stuff of life, to sustain itself and future generations, as well as the capacity to grow into enormous things with root systems that extend far and wide.

Our apple trees arrived that morning, wrapped in burlap, a cluster of thin whips bound together by twine. I remember being a bit incredulous when receiving instructions that the whips were to be planted fifteen feet from each other, especially given that they were not but a few feet in length themselves. Did it really need to be fifteen feet? It seemed to me that ten feet would have been sufficient, and with that kind of spacing, we could plant three trees for every two at fifteen feet—that's a 50 percent increase! Proud of my productivity mindset, I approached Dr. Takekuma with my brilliant idea, and it was met with a very simple and straightforward answer.

No.

It was the kind of "no" that made it clear that your suggestion was not worthy of consideration.

I was unoffended by the gruffness of the reply, more curious as to why my idea had provoked such clarity. It was not until some days later that my reflections helped me to see that my suggestion to maximize production was not only ill-advised; it perfectly illustrated the difference between a plant-based and a soil-based approach to farming.

First, my time horizon was short (I was already planning my return to the United States), and due to my inexperience as a farmer, I lacked imagination. I was focused on what I could physically see and touch—an open field and a bundle of bare-root trees—and how, in that moment, I could get more of those whips into the ground such that, at the end of the day, I could look out over the field and claim victory for planting so many trees. Never mind the crowded spacing and if and how they might grow toward their fullest potential; those were concerns for another day and, in fact, for another person to deal with.

Second, what the "victory" of the number of planted trees above the surface belied was that the tight spacing would eventually impair the root growth and compromise long-term sustainability. Even with healthy soil conditions for growth, such trees would inevitably require external inputs to survive through their maturation—and be pushed to compete with each other for resources, largely due to their closer proximity.

Along these lines, I could understand Dr. Takekuma's "no" as protection of the spaciousness that these young trees would need to thrive. It was not just space, but the right amount of space, that was so important to tend to.

Furthermore, it was my failure to see the connection between space *and* time that kept me from seeing (or even imagining) the value and importance of spaciousness. It wasn't until some years later, in my own leadership (and through working with other leaders), that I could see the clear parallels with organizational life, where we often only have the immediate-term view in our perspective.

In the early days of leading my own organization, I did not have Dr. Takekuma by my side to kindly, but firmly, tell me "no" when my production-heavy ideas and interventions were short-sighted, naive, and destined to burn myself (and others) out. I did not have the awareness (and in all honesty, the humility) to choose spaciousness. I even felt embarrassed or ashamed when I felt worn out or had to take a pause.

It was not until I connected the lessons of soil compaction to the challenges of leadership that I was able to grow and deepen my approach to work (and life). Intentionally building in fallow time for myself and disconnecting from things (and people) that I knew to be purveyors of compaction. Embracing my tendencies toward quiet and stillness and renewing my relationship to them—not as characteristics of a leader being on the sidelines, but of a leader who is focused on growing the deeper roots of purpose.

I am now at the point in my life and in my leadership where I know that if I do not have spaciousness and the forces of social compaction are too great, I will not be the kind of person (and leader) I aspire to be.

Only when you allow spaciousness can new ideas or opportunities, new roots (and shoots), really begin to grow.

SCALING UP VS. ROOTING DOWN

"How are you going to bring your work to scale?"

It is a question that has been asked of me so many times from donors and investors that I can't even remember the first time I heard it. And like many business owners and entrepreneurs, I quickly developed an almost robotic response to imply both that there is a growth plan and that such growth is an important pursuit. It was not until a particularly profound reflective practice, which came as a result of frustrations with myself and a nagging sense that I was parroting a line rather than being authentic, that I realized that the soil had even more to teach me.

By now we have well established how farmers regularly think beyond the present and into the future. It is a visionary act of hope and trust: hope that what you plant will yield a rich harvest, and trust that how you have prepared and tended the earth creates the best possible conditions for growth. In my work doing leadership development with individuals, we are often asked for metrics of success, encouraged to point to tangible outcomes such as number of participants or new organizations created or funding received. Yet, as we know, the work is not simply about growing plants—our first job is to cultivate a healthy and thriving soil.

Just as I learned on Dr. Takekuma's farm to think about spaciousness through the lens of multiple time horizons, spacing trees with an eye not just to immediate yield, but to long-term growth, I began to see how in my nonfarm work I needed to think carefully about the number of program participants and what was the "right spacing" to ensure deep root growth and long-term health and viability of both the leaders and their organizations. Just counting heads was not the right measure of success (even when that is the metric funders requested). When I started to see the work with individuals as a soil-building proposition and how the initial trainings my organization provided were just the start of a longer-term connection, it unlocked a perspective that brought the tangible and the intangible into union. I came to see that our approach to scaling up is primarily with the individuals we work with. These individuals, through their positions and commitment to social impact in their communities and countries, are working directly with hundreds, if not thousands, of beneficiaries. They are the thriving trees, who set hundreds of fruits and yield dozens of new scions.

Therefore, if they are to continue to produce fruit and impact lives, what is most important is the strength and depth of their root systems. Put differently, what matters most is not scaling up and out, but rooting down and deep. When we pay attention to spaciousness and the spaces in between, we create the conditions for transformational and long-term growth.

The Space for Leadership in US-Based Global Development Work

"Spaciousness has been an important learning, as it has enabled a greater flow of energy and regenerative resource exchange in my life and in my leadership approach. Making intentional space, be it in the form of a sabbatical or creating times of gentle *being* amidst an oversupply of *doings* during daily life, has been really important for me. Amid the cacophony of our fast world, without this spaciousness, it is hard to listen to the voice of the spirit that is vital in the process of inner and outer transformations. I took major (and hard) leadership transition decisions that called for deep courage in body, mind, and spirit. As a result, I transitioned from a glamorized, singular nonprofit-cofounder identity to step into a wholeness that combines my lifelong climate justice work with my creative callings as an immigrant artist who believes in the transformative power of art to heal our private, collective, planetary lives. Embodying wholeness in a fragmented world is a gift that I courageously share with the world today."

Neha Misra (USA)
Creator, Neha Misra Studio
Global Ambassador, Remote Energy
Cofounder, Solar Sister (Transitioned)

Creating Spaciousness in DR Congo

"As a leader in AGIR-RDC and an activist in the province of North Kivu, my context has been marked by wars, insecurities, injustices, and human rights violations for the past decade. In such circumstances, I have focused on two crucial aspects. Firstly, I have worked on building personal and collective resilience among my colleagues, fellow activists, and the younger generation. In an environment where urgent needs demand relentless activism, it becomes essential to act beyond our limits. However, I have also learned the discipline of saying no to create more spaciousness—a valuable lesson and a significant challenge. I continually work on myself to remain an activist for life while learning to set boundaries. Creating an environment that promotes spaciousness in DR Congo is vital. Just as compacted soil inhibits plant growth, overwhelming schedules and excessive workloads hinder the delivery of quality services. AGIR-RDC, the organization I am part of, is dedicated to empowering vulnerable Congolese individuals and acting as a force multiplier. We prioritize spaciousness in our operations, establishing clear pathways and protocols to streamline workflows and minimize unnecessary chaos. By fostering a culture of collaboration and teamwork, we ensure that responsibilities are shared, allowing each team member to thrive in their role. Embracing the concept of spaciousness in our leadership approach has yielded remarkable improvements in our ability to empower the vulnerable and deliver impactful services. We recognize that, like life itself, growth requires space, and as leaders, we are committed to cultivating that space for AGIR-RDC and the communities we serve."

Modestine Etoy (Democratic Republic of Congo)
Executive Director
AGIR-RDC

REFLECTION

As you complete this chapter, I invite you to take a moment to pause and reflect on the following Inquiries.

- How does soil compaction show up in your life and/or leadership?
- What are some things causing soil compaction in your life? In your work?
    - e.g., the stack of activities in your life and work, such as meetings, reporting, shopping, cleaning, caretaking, etc.
- How do you participate in causing this soil compaction?

- e.g., mindlessly doing these activities because it feels urgent, because it is necessary, because it feels like more is better, squeezing back-to-back meetings into every gap in your schedule, etc.
- What is preventing you from creating more spaciousness?
    - e.g., being judged, upsetting others, loss of opportunities, feeling like you have to know or do everything asked of you, etc.
- What would be possible if there was more spaciousness?
    - e.g., more peace of mind, time with family, ability to take on an important project that always gets pushed to the back burner, better health, etc.
- What do you need for this to happen?
    - e.g., better boundaries, time away from work, more or better help at home or work, etc.

CHAPTER 7

Roots

Mind the fruits.
Manage the shoots.
Lead from roots.

Roots, and the soil in which they are planted, matter.

Summon the language of roots and you had better have something worth saying.

In the canon of metaphors, roots are used to evoke a sense of purpose, connectedness, and inner resolve. The root—or roots in general—are invoked when we want to express that we are going deep.

Yet a root is not simply a root.

Some gently creep horizontally just beneath the surface, while others penetrate deep into the earth. Some are fleshy and enlarged, while others are thin and stringy. Some attach themselves to other plants and act as parasites, while others, even in their old age, can serve as a conduit, delivering water, nutrients, and information to other parts of the plant—even, in some cases, to other plants in their area.

A root is not simply a root.

This lesson I learned early on the farm offers a different way of thinking about how metaphors consciously and unconsciously shape our capacities to make meaning of the present and imagine into the future.

GRASS ROOTS

Take, for example, the commonly used metaphor of the *grass roots*. Often used in politics and the social sector to evoke images of community and "real" people working to create change, it is typically set up as a foil to large institutions and dominant sociopolitical or economic icons; it implies a certain on-the-ground knowledge of reality that is unattainable by larger actors. It is not unfamiliar for those involved in social-change work to evaluate the authenticity and legitimacy of others based on their perceived proximity to these grass roots.

I know because I have lived and spoken this for my entire adult life.

Grasses are monocotyledons, including all the major grains (rice, wheat, maize, etc.), forage grasses, sugarcane, bamboos, bananas, and plantains. The family name may be a mouthful, but its members are largely responsible for feeding humanity. Generally speaking, at least in agriculture, the grassy monocots appear to understand that their destiny resides above the surface and in numbers. Their work is for all to see.

Most of these grasses have what are called fibrous root systems: located close to the soil surface in a dense network of similar-sized roots that make up for their lack of depth with strength in numbers. Anyone who has tried to replace grass in their garden knows that shallow roots in community are not to be underestimated. At the same time, the roots of grasses are largely superficial. They find strength in their underground network, but their survival is reliant on the happenings above the surface, things generally out of their control. Grass roots are not particularly equipped to handle that kind of change.

So in the context of leadership, the idea of grass roots is not particularly helpful. We need a different kind of root that evokes other dimensions of our humanity. One that draws attention to depth and purpose. One that pushes us to move beyond the top layer and, perhaps, even beyond comfort in community and familiar language.

Let's turn to a root that can dig deep to sustain so much activity above the surface. As a metaphor for the elements of leadership, it anchors and enables our interventions in life-giving ways that promote connection.

THE TAPROOT

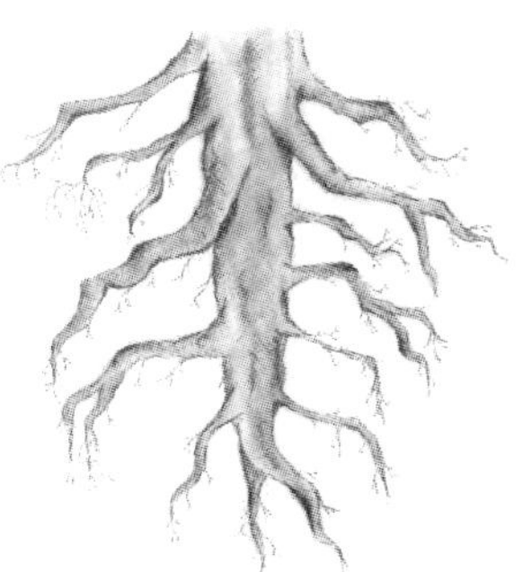

Unlike the fibrous, clustered root systems of grasses, taproot systems have a main, large, central root that grows down vertically into the earth, and off which smaller roots can grow laterally. A taproot drives deep into soil and sometimes, as in the case of carrots and beets, serves as the core storage organ for the plant, accumulating nutrients with every millimeter it plumbs. The strength of the taproot is such that for some plants, even if some of the smaller roots are harvested or snapped off, they can grow back. Usually the first root to develop in a plant's embryonic stage, as the taproot grows, it can penetrate deep into the soil, allowing the plant to access water and nutrients that may not be available near the surface. Some species of trees have taproots that extend several meters into the ground. The taproot allows plants to survive and thrive in a variety of different environments.

A taproot means business.

When I dig down to get to the taproot, I do so not to supplant the work at the grass roots but to enlarge the framing, to consider them both/and of fostering a collective *and* tending to the unique taproots in each individual. Staying at the grassroots level is an invitation to oversolving or thinking that just because you have penetrated a bit beneath the surface, you have a sense of the true depth of a situation. But as Reflective Practice reveals, iterative practice takes you deeper into the multifaceted contexts of a situation and is not a "one and done," because you are trying to understand, not just fix, solve, and resolve.

Taproots provide stability and enable absorption. As we can learn from natural systems, when the taproot is strong, so, too, is the tree. The point in introducing the taproot is not to override other root-based metaphors like grass roots, nor to encourage you on a road to isolation, but rather to emphasize the importance of purpose and the foundational "why" of our work, leadership, and lives. The taproot is the conduit that provides connection to what matters most deeply. And it is this connection that sustains you—as is the case with plants—when conditions are challenging and resources scarce.

GOBO

When it comes to food, while flowering plants deliver us goodness through their fruits but do not give their lives in the process, root crops offer the very foundation of their being to provide sustenance to others. Unlike the crops that deliver in the light of day, carefully managed so that they can produce season after season, the root crop is dug up, displaced from the darkness, and cut off from its capacity to mature, even as it seeks to fulfill its purpose to persist.

We can, therefore, say that the root crop—carrots, icicle radishes, beets, parsnips, etc.—is asked to do what many other flowering plants are not: to abandon its purpose as a perennial in service to an annual outcome.

But as is the case in life, not all root crops are created equal. From the affable carrot to the dramatic beet to the elegant daikon, there are all kinds of characters beneath the surface.

And on an autumn day in Japan, I first met one of the lesser known but most impressive of the edible roots: burdock.

Burdock, called *gobo* in Japanese, is, in fact, my favorite of all vegetables, due to its capacity for depth, expansion, and the transformation of compacted earth. Most Westerners have never tasted burdock, much less seen a burdock plant. With its elephant-ear leaves and thick stems, above ground it resembles a wild, overgrown chard plant; but it is underneath the surface where its true power resides.

Earlier on this day, Dr. Takekuma had a deep, machine-dug trench placed alongside a twenty-five-meter row of gobo that were ready for harvest. The work exposed several feet beneath the surface and resulted in a four-foot-deep furrow, flanked by two mounds of displaced earth.

Jumping into the trench, I took instructions on how to properly uproot a gobo root so that it does not snap off at the midpoint, which would leave its commercial value deep in the soil. Like many things on a farm, the instructions are simple—in this case, pull with an even force and at an angle consistent with the root's growth trajectory—but successful execution requires some repetition and failure.

It is said that gobo roots can travel tens of meters in every direction and that they can grow in some of the most inhospitable soils. The thin, whip-like tendrils find their way through clay and compaction in a manner that would be impossible for other plants. With every extension and root hair, they absorb trace minerals and nutrients from the earth while seeking deeper sources of aerobic energy.

Through the process, the gobo carves out pathways in the compacted earth and makes space for other ingredients of life—air and water in particular—to reinhabit and help the soil breathe again. In this way gobo plants open up the spaces in the larger contexts that give life to all.

There are few plants I love as much as the gobo.

BECOMING ROOT-BOUND

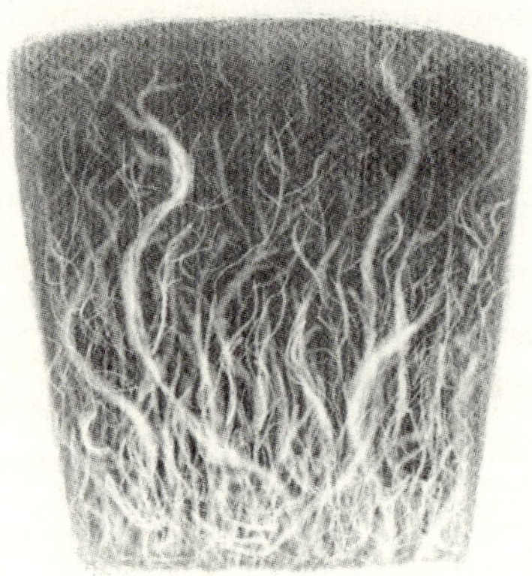

I have found that one of the most resonant aspects of the root-leadership metaphor is the phenomenon of a plant becoming root-bound.

A plant becomes root-bound when its root systems run out of space. This occurs when a plant is grown in a container (not in open soil), and if the plant is not moved to a larger pot when it begins to become root-bound, its growth will be stunted. If you have ever repotted a plant later than you should have, you know what it looks like for a plant to be root-bound—a gnarled, dense mass of roots that allows for little or no space for further growth.

To be root-bound is to be stuck in a context where it is impossible to grow, and all attempts to do so are met with a resistance that cannot be overcome.

To be root-bound means that, over time, the efforts to grow and find nutrients in the soil will be limited so that the only option is to go inward and be resigned to the size of your container.

To be root-bound is to adjust and adapt to the pot that you are in, even though it is ill fitting and you lack the proper space to grow into your full potential.

On my farm, we used to start crops by first direct seeding into flats (seed trays) and then, once there were small seedlings, planting those seedlings into the ground. This strategy was not only much more efficient and precise than scattering seeds directly into the soil and thinning the sprouts, but also helped to reduce the risk of crop loss due to pests. It was always exciting to know that in just one small flat of seedlings there might be a quarter hectare of plants being raised.

And at the same time, it was clear that the time these plants needed to spend in the flats was minimal—with a one-inch width and two-inch depth, the small cells that held the germination process were hardly the place for any plant to reach its full potential. We knew that once the sprouts had reached a certain size, they would need to be set out into the field. And if we did not time it right, they would become root-bound and/or struggle to adapt when set out into the soil.

So there was a finite, often narrow, window for success: if we did not act soon enough, the plants would struggle to take root in their new home, even if the soil was as healthy as could be.

Plants that had become overly conditioned to their tight surroundings would be unable to grow, even when we moved them to a larger space. They needed the protection of the seed flats to thrive in their first weeks, but then, at a critical time, they needed room to grow.

Organizations also often need a well-bounded space to begin with, so that they can develop with all due care, but a key task for a leader is knowing when to transfer that organization (or seedling) to a larger field. Do it too soon, and the organization (or organism) might be overwhelmed by predators or unable to find nourishment; do it too late, and you may find your organization is root-bound and struggles to grow in its more open space.

Over my years of working with leaders and managing people, I often have thought about my experience with root-bound plants and how it can inform how and when change and transition need to occur. As we have discussed in this book, people, like plants, need the right conditions—the right soil—in order to grow, thrive, and pursue their full potential. And when those contexts are overly constrained and bounded, the lack of space means that those roots—the stuff of curiosity, discovery, and personal and professional growth—can become a tangled mass of immobility. And while above the surface the plant still looks relatively healthy, its frozen root system suggests that energies are in a degenerative state of being.

There are countless examples of people in contexts (jobs, positions, relationships, etc.) where they are root-bound, trying to grow in situations that once promoted growth and sustenance but have become spaces of restraint. This can especially be the case for founders and entrepreneurs as over time their organizations and businesses become ill-fitted pots where their roots have nowhere to go.

And, unfortunately, as with trying to replant a root-bound plant, if there is insufficient care given in the transfer, even in a new space that plant will stay tangled in its root ball as if it is still in its old container. It doesn't know how to grow into the available new space.

For a root-bound plant to be able to thrive again, the roots need to be carefully teased out of mass and prepared for the new space, so that the plant can overcome the inevitable shock of a new environment.

And so it is with people: root-boundness can be overcome with the introduction of new space, but it requires close attention and care.

Simply picking up an organization, project, or even a leader from one space and plopping it/them into new ground is not enough. Without care, we can unintentionally transfer or even replicate the previously learned constraints.

People can become root-bound when we harden our perspectives and become more fixed in our assumptions. As a leader, you might find yourself (root-)bound by your ideas and frameworks of leadership, learned or developed in one space, place, or time, perhaps from role models that do not align with your approach and sense of self.

Perhaps the root-boundedness is due to long-running stories that you tell yourself about what processes, attitudes, or approaches are required—even if they feel wrong or destructive—in order to achieve particular outcomes.

Whatever it might be, the animating, core question is: are you still growing?

And if the answer is "no," then what can you do about it?

DEEP WATERING

One of the most challenging and important lessons that I learned on the farm was how to water. What at first appeared to be the most straightforward of tasks was, like so many things in the realm of the stewardship of life, full of simple and profound practices.

For my entire life, I believed that to water *a* plant meant to literally water *the* plant.

Some of my earliest memories are with my grandmother in her garden, acting like a little god, making rain from the spout of my cracked watering can and showering the flowers with the torrential force of a flash flood. There was some aesthetic pleasure in the glistening leaves and a sense that I had imparted life into these thirsty creatures.

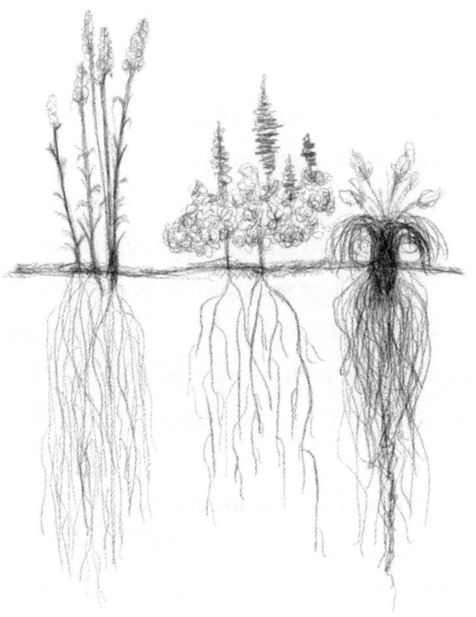

Yet in the same way that people do not take showers to hydrate, so, too, is the case for many crops.

And so I learned this lesson very early in my life on the farm: we do not water plants; we water the soil.

Watering the soil means tending to the conditions under which plant roots can and will absorb moisture. It means thinking about how the patterns and strategies of watering can shape plant health and resilience. It means knowing some things, while also trusting that much of what needs to happen is beyond our view.

Deep watering is an approach to irrigation designed to ensure the moisture penetrates far deeper than just the first few inches of topsoil. Deep watering seeks to reduce the evaporation at the soil's surface by watering longer and less frequently in order to coax the plants' roots to greater depths as they seek hydration. This results in plants with stronger foundations and that are less prone to the kinds of stresses that come as the result of moisture deficiency.

In short, the practice of deep watering results in greater resilience by focusing on the depth of roots.

Reflective practice is a form of deep watering. Through reflective practice, you can reach more deeply into the soil to locate more sustenance. Reflective practice will help you bring new insights, which have been buried far beneath your actions, to the surface, so that you can consider whether and how they serve you and your purpose, how and whether they inform your actions.

In the case of deep watering, the roots are following the moisture. And, as farmers, we develop an approach to thoughtfully challenge the plant's root system to go beyond the offerings of the near-surface soil and seek sustenance at the deeper levels. That stress—not excessive but intentional—results in a plant that is ready for a wider range of experiences. A plant that is better equipped to thrive.

The roots need both the water at deeper levels *and* the lack of water at the surface level for a result of greater resilience.

And so, too, it is with leadership.

These deepening practices will challenge you. You may have to dig through some calcifications and rocky soil, but if you, like the gobo, push through, you will make new space for yourself and for others to grow.

Roots, and the soil in which they are planted, matter.

Deeply Rooted in Northern India

"Learning from the wisdom of natural systems has been an essential piece of how I have come to lead my organization. My organization's work in drought mitigation, healthcare, and sustainable development in the Thar Desert of northern India embodies the concept of roots. Just like the diverse types of roots in nature, our integrated approach goes beyond addressing the water crisis and extends to transforming lives through education, healthcare, microfinance, and advocacy for vulnerable communities. In my leadership journey, I have come to appreciate the significance of the taproot. When I do, I don't dismiss the importance of grassroots efforts, but instead expand my perspective to encompass both collective action and individual empowerment. I am able to recognize that truly understanding complex situations requires going beyond surface-level solutions and engaging in reflective practice. Our emphasis on purpose and the foundational "why" of our work strengthens our stability and enables us to absorb knowledge, grow, and create a lasting impact in the lives of those we serve."

Prakash Tyagi (India)
Executive Director
GRAVIS

Deep Watering in Malawi

"In our organization, we prioritize the development of strong roots by focusing on essential elements such as inclusive teaching methodologies, specialized resources, and accessible infrastructure. By addressing these foundational aspects, we ensure that children have the necessary support and opportunities to flourish. We also recognize the significance of individualized approaches that cater to the unique needs and strengths of each child, enabling them to establish deep roots in their education. Just as deep watering goes beyond merely wetting the surface of the soil, our approach to education transcends superficial learning. We strive to provide children with a strong, inclusive foundation by creating an environment that fosters deep-rooted knowledge, understanding, and skills. We believe that if these children start right, they are definitely starting strong."

Patience Musiwa-Mkandawire (Malawi)
Founder and Executive Director
Fount for Nations

REFLECTION

As you complete this chapter, I invite you to take a moment to pause and reflect on the following Inquiries.

- How would you describe the nature of the root systems in your community, organization, business, or institution?
- How does the current condition of the soil in your work context influence root growth?
- How would you describe the difference between a grassroots-oriented and a taproot-oriented approach to leadership in your context or organization?

- What is the taproot of your personal leadership?
- What is the taproot of your organization or business?
- Are there any circumstances in your life and/or work where you feel root-bound? If so, why?
- How does the concept of deep watering show up (or not) in your work and your life?

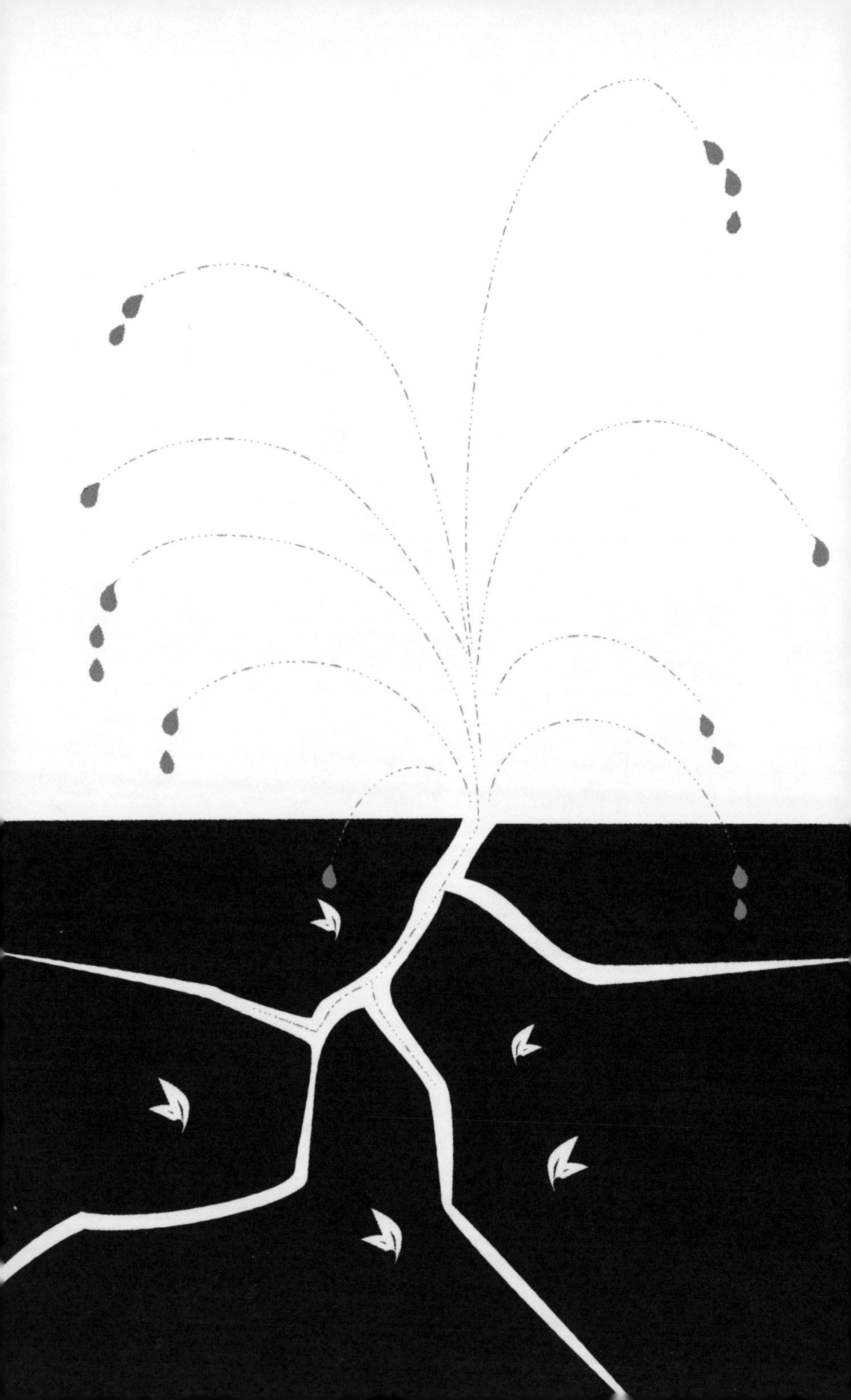

CHAPTER 8

Well-Being

Beneath the surface
lives the universe.
Life in all its potential
in one, small
scoop of
earth.
In every moment here
are acts of God.
Powerful forces
exercise their skill:
to metabolize and transform
energy.
Here, life is not a construct
nor an imaginary or riddle.
It is simply
a practice
of purpose.
Beneath the surface
lives the universe.
Sustained by
the space to breathe.
The immeasurable gaps,
ten billion on a pinhead,

pathways
where nutrient
flows
and
roots
will grow.
Beneath the surface
lives the universe.
Beware the unconscious fool.
Heel above, driving
billions of microscopic displacements,
suffocating and crushing
the spaces in between.
Pathways for root growth
cut off by
an epic annihilation
under a
crisp sneaker.
The surface above,
merely a reflection
of what lies beneath.
And there are
no healthy shoots
without
strong roots.
It is, therefore,
the breathing below
that gives life to the
growth above.
Beneath the surface
lives the universe.

Regenerative farming is about the promotion of health and well-being.

Whether at the macro level of protecting biodiversity or reducing the negative impacts of agriculture on climate, the meso level of promoting greater connections between farmers and their communities and economic opportunity, or the micro level of soil health and fertility, sustainable farming is a holistic approach built on the understanding that relationships form the foundation of healthy systems.

In earlier chapters we covered how Dr. Takekuma cultivated the conditions for growth and transformation on his farm by building a soil fed by relationship and connection.

In this chapter we will apply a soil-building approach to something that may sound familiar but begs for a new approach that prioritizes roots over fruits and the transformational over the temporary: well-being.

WILTING

"You are like a plant without water."

My colleague peered at me over her glasses with a quizzical eyebrow lift and a piercing stare.

"You are wilting. How are you nourishing yourself?"

I was stunned.

Was it so obvious that I was burning the candle at both ends, frustrated at work and tense at home?

Apparently, it was.

I prided myself on being able to compartmentalize and draw firm emotional boundaries in order to present a professional demeanor (which often meant being positive and energetic). This was not my best friend or my family seeing through the facade; this was a colleague from another organization with whom I was trying to build a partnership. And, if I'm being honest, I might have brushed off the comment from friends or family (I might have thought—they don't understand how hard I *have* to work!), but from this woman, who is herself a powerhouse and who wanted us to succeed together, I had to listen.

Yet still I lied.

I lied in a way that we all do and without a hint of shame. I lied in a way that you probably have done several times already today.

I said that I was "fine."

Fortunately (for me) this was not just anyone making these observations. She was two decades my senior, someone whose leadership and life's work I greatly respected, and who I knew had been through a number of struggles with family and work. She was not someone who was going to let my evasive answer slide by.

"C'mon, let's be real here. How are you doing? What are you doing to nourish yourself?"

Perhaps it was the kind and firm way she re-asked the questions. Perhaps it was that I was coming to our meeting with little rest and an empty stomach. Perhaps it was because I had already lost track of the day of the week and the time of the year. Perhaps it was because I sensed she could relate.

But it forced me, with love and care, to face a reality I had been denying and certainly not acknowledged aloud:

"I'm not doing well."

Finally.

Honesty.

WELL-BEING IS A MUST

If you're wilting on the surface, your soil dried out long ago. It is, therefore, long past time to regenerate your taproot by building a practice of deep watering—a practice of well-being.

From a soil-building perspective, well-being is about creating the space and time to have a more purposeful relationship with ourselves and with our lives. Ongoing well-being requires attention both to your relationships to others and to the world around you. But in this chapter, we will focus on your most essential relationship for a successful leadership practice: your relationship with yourself.

Well-being is surely an end in itself, but for most leaders (really, for most everyone), commitment to well-being takes discipline. For all of the emphasis on how inspiration and passion ignite leadership, it is truly commitment and discipline that allow us to endure. Leaders are regularly pulled in multiple directions with limited time and space. A commitment to well-being can seem like a nice-to-have, an add-on, a when-I-have-time.

But if I have learned anything in my two decades of working with leaders and organizations all over the world, it is that a well-being practice is essential to leadership practice.

Put differently, a commitment to well-being is not a nice-to-have; it is a must do.

I find the best way to ensure leaders honor a commitment to well-being—theirs, their team's, their organization's—is to anchor it in purpose. Ask yourself: Why is my well-being important to me? To my team? To my organization?

WELL-BEING VS. SELF-CARE

Self-care promotes doing things for yourself to feel good or positive. While this is not a negative thing, the impact can be temporary, because the self-care frame does not ask whether those activities strengthen your systems and/or patterns of behavior or shift your state of being in a sustained way. They are usually focused on relaxing (a good thing) or looking good to feel good (fine, as far as it goes, if that works for you). Self-care activities are not skill building and they tend not to be designed to help you recalibrate for the long term.

Well-being practices are more about preparing you, both internally and externally, to access your full capabilities with more ease. It's about the work of awareness. It is not a one-time activity that a person does to feel good, but a discipline one follows with intentionality to create a habit that develops more deeply rooted resources.

Put into the parlance of the Soil of Leadership: Self-Care is for the plants—your presentation, your maintenance, your ability to get from one day to the next. Well-being is about the soil—your deeper sense of purpose, your ongoing commitment to yourself and the reasons why you do the work, your investment in the long term and the depth of the roots you want to grow.

Self-Care vs. Well-Being

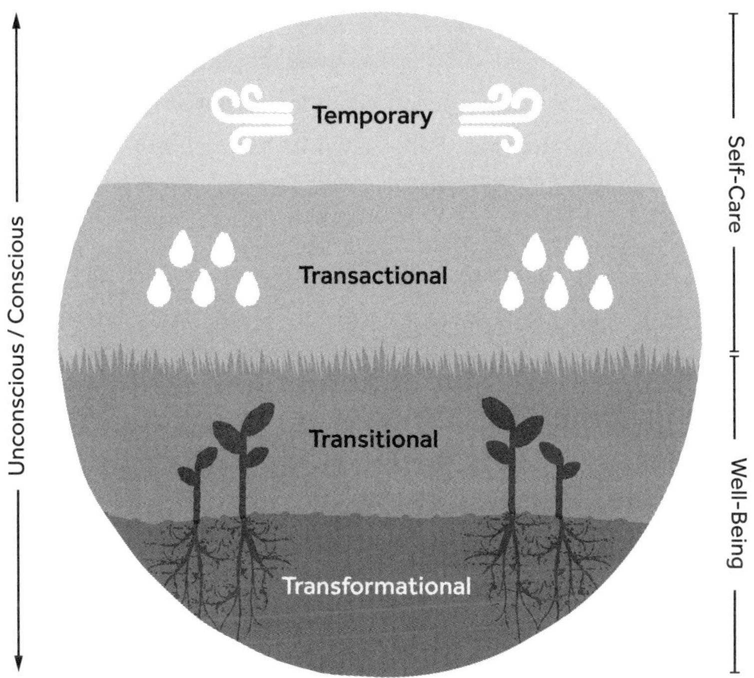

In this diagram we have four states of being: temporary, transactional, transitional, and transformational. Self-care activities are temporary and transactional. Well-being practices are transitional and transformational. The spectrum of unconscious to conscious spans the entire lot.

Temporary

This is the realm of self-care that consists of short-lived and irregular activities. While, generally speaking, there is nothing inherently wrong or bad about activities that fall under this category, they tend to be palliative measures that are often toward the unconscious (tuning out) end of the spectrum. Some activities that fall into this realm include binge-watching media, watching your favorite sports team play, getting a massage, and meeting friends for drinks. All wonderful and important in their own right, but in this model, they have relatively weak impact on long-term well-being. These temporary actions feel good and have their place, but do not mistake them for a commitment to well-being.

Transactional

A number of very important activities fall under this category, including things that you likely need to function well, and they have tangible positive results. You gain some specific, often important benefits *in exchange* for attending to them. Some examples include regular physical exercise, sufficient sleep, a balanced and nutritious diet, social connections and support, and access to healthcare. Without regular physical activity, our physical health can deteriorate. A lack of sleep can lead to fatigue, cognitive impairment, and mood disturbances. Poor nutrition can lead to deficiencies and a weakened immune system. Social isolation can increase the risk of mental health issues, while not having access to healthcare can result in untreated illnesses and a decline in overall health. Therefore, it's essential to prioritize these transactional activities in our lives to maintain our overall health and well-being.

Transitional

These practices are animated by a sense of purpose and real commitment. These are actions you undertake on a regular basis because you know that they contribute positively to your well-being. These practices move beyond the basics of sleep, food, and fundamental physical movement. They are actions you undertake out of a dedication to your well-being and ongoing development.

The demarcation line between transactional activities and transitional practices is a matter of awareness and the conscious intentionality behind them. This may seem like a small matter, but it is the essential ingredient for turning a mindless activity into a mindful practice, and it is the source from which long-term, more sustainable leadership that centers well-being flows.

Transformational

Deliberate, thoughtful, grounded practices that layer over time to generate a deeply rooted capacity for well-being. In my own life, I have learned that to be in this realm takes practice, vulnerability, care, commitment, and, most of all, discipline. It is not easy. But I have also learned that when I am not pointed in the direction of transformational well-being, I cannot truly inspire and create systems and structures with integrity and purpose. In this realm I am consistently reminded that well-being is a practice and a process. It is not solely a destination. There is no perfection, no achieving, no finishing or fixing. There is only commitment to yourself, your heart, and your deeper self.

Much has been said in the fields of leadership development and self-care about the power of mindset in shaping everything from wealth to health. Many books and/or "thought leaders" will tell you that being able to adjust your mindset is a core capacity. It is a core capacity in the practice of "personal empowerment" and tilting our lives toward the outcomes we seek.

But just because it may feel a part of exaggerated and overblown ballyhoo, does not make it untrue.

Buried under the layers of ego-oriented interventions, shaky permission systems, and persuasive messengers rests a powerful truth: shifting perception is the threshold to transformation.

Self-care may be all the rage, but it is usually a precursor to a sales pitch: just take some time for yourself (with this product) and your problem(s) will be solved! I am not saying those products or interventions don't have their place. If you love your spa, then go to the spa! If you love your meditation app, use it! But just know that there is still a distance between that action and your well-being. That distance is bridged by intention.

WORK-LIFE BALANCE

Let's take a moment to discuss the elephant in the room: work-life balance.

This is a framing I fundamentally reject.

The idea of work-life balance is based on the assumption that work is not inextricably a part of life.

If you work solely to earn money and nothing else, perhaps you can treat it as something that can be balanced. But if you are driven to be a leader, chances are good that your work is not simply about a paycheck. If your work is your vocation, a calling, or something that you seek to do with dedication, then work-life balance as an idea that simply cannot exist for you, because your work is a part of your life. So to try to cleave your work from your life is a false premise.

The phrase "work-life balance" implies work and life can be balanced on a scale, removing a few hours from one side and adding a few to the other to achieve that sought-after sense of equilibrium. Instead of aiming for balance, it's better to view work and life as two distinct things that are nested within each other, with a relationship between them that needs to be understood and more consciously tended—not simply by counting hours, but by ensuring that your unique and individual wants and needs are being appropriately nourished.

Work-life balance is not something to strive for. We cannot balance the unbalanceable and expect it to be the solution for a better life.

As Simple as Brushing Your Teeth

- Why do you brush your teeth?
- When did you learn to brush your teeth?
- How did you learn? Who taught you?
- How do you feel when you don't brush your teeth?
- What is necessary to ensure that you brush your teeth?
- Why is it so hard for you to adopt and implement a well-being practice—something that you know, without question, is good for you?
- What would it mean for your life if you were to integrate a well-being practice into your daily routine, the same way that you have with brushing your teeth?

YOUR DEEP WATERING AND WELL-BEING PRACTICE

When it comes to well-being, I have learned that commitment has to come from within. If you don't feel it, you won't accomplish it. But there are ways to grow soil and stronger roots even if you start with a shallow, root-bound mess. There is a process that provides a structure and scaffolding toward greater well-being for leaders.

This is called the Perennial Well-Being Practice.

The core tenets of this exercise are to get you to identify a practice and to help you develop a strategy that cultivates the conditions for you to successfully integrate it into your regular life. Importantly, as the word perennial implies, it is also a long-term, recurring practice.

The Perennial Well-Being Practice is a self-selected, ongoing activity that positively contributes to and restores your overall sense of well-being—emotionally, physically, and perhaps even spiritually. It is an essential element in building a more generative and restorative leadership that is grounded and whole. It enables leaders to have the time and space to come into deeper connection with themselves and with others (relationship), and thus pursue work more deeply rooted to what matters most to them.

Your relationship with yourself requires time plus space to thrive so you can grow your soil.

This practice helps you build a foundation that will set you up to thrive. It is about forming a set of habits that you do regularly and improve over time in order to experience its full benefits, charting a course that cares for one's mental, emotional, physical, and spiritual health.

The key to success will be discipline and commitment, and yes, it may not be easy, but nothing worthwhile ever is.

Deep watering takes time.

Please download the Perennial Well-Being Practice worksheet at soilleadership.com and begin the process of identifying a practice for you. On the worksheet you will also find tips for how to overcome obstacles and the kinds of inevitable resistance that come with any form of significant life change.

Some important points to remember as you embark on this journey:

- Commit to prioritizing your Well-Being Practice over a forty-day period.
- A lot of what we are trying to do through this process is to normalize activities and make them a part of your regular daily/weekly routine(s).
- You are not committing to doing this one activity for the rest of your life. In some ways, at this point, it is less about the activity itself and more about you learning how to design and execute a process that has beneficial outcomes for your health and well-being.
- Repetition builds regularity.
- Stacking wins builds important momentum.
- Extrinsic motivation can be catalytic in the short term, but it is rarely a good long-term solution.

Cultivating Well-Being in Kenya

"Well-being has been the biggest lesson for me. My organization runs medical facilities and has created over fifty safe spaces for maternal child health in difficult, hard-to-reach communities. This means I am overstretched. I am overworked and the demands of the community are more than I can bear sometimes. My work often takes a toll on my well-being. Unfortunately, for women, especially for strong women, nobody asks you if you are okay or if you need support. As a strong person, you're expected to hold the world together, you're supposed to hold the sky. With a team of over thirty staff and over three hundred community health workers, often it feels like twenty-four hours is not enough. However, I have come to understand that for me to help my community, I need to make sure my well-being is tended to. I ensure my well-being is a priority by being conscious of identifying and reassessing my habits. And really being conscious of when I'm about to hit a certain point, so that I don't wait to hit rock bottom anymore, like I used to. I now know when I'm heading in this direction, and I start looking after myself and being more intentional in how much time I am giving to certain projects, how I delegate, how I even engage my family members in helping me to solve and to help out in some of those responsibilities. Because I realized that if I'm not here tomorrow, everybody will just go on with their work, they will just go on with life. And I won't be here to enjoy my life, and I can't say nobody helped me, because I never told them that I was dying."

Wendo Sahar Aszed (Kenya)
Chief Executive Officer
Dandelion Africa

Modeling Well-Being in El Salvador

"Tending to my own well-being can be challenging, as there are many demands pulling me in different directions. However, through the discipline of a Well-Being Practice consisting of intentional exercise and mindful breathing, I have found a way to reconnect with myself. This practice has helped me rediscover myself and my capacity for love. Without it, I felt disconnected and lost. At first, making time for my Practice was difficult, as people often have high expectations of my time and energy. I felt like I had to be perfect, always available, and constantly fighting to maintain my energy and wisdom. It was exhausting. But as my Practice solidified, so did its impact. My colleagues and partners started noticing the difference in how I showed up at work. Even during turbulent times, they noticed I was not getting as stressed as I would before. I was calm and grounded. Because I was modeling well-being, I knew I would be able to create a culture of well-being for my organization. I had the language and a structure for it. As I hear distressing statistics about the number of leaders who struggle with burnout and mental health issues, I am grateful that I have this process."

Lucy Luna Guzmán (El Salvador)
Executive Director
ASAPROSAR

REFLECTION

As you complete this chapter, I invite you to take a moment to pause and reflect on the following inquiries.

- Remember that self-care is a plant-based proposition: your presentation, your maintenance, your ability to get from one day to the next. Well-being is a soil-based proposition: your deeper sense of purpose, your ongoing commitment to yourself and the reasons why you do the work, your investment in the long term and the depth of the roots you want to grow. Think about the things you explicitly do for yourself: How many are self-care interventions and how many are well-being practices? Do you currently have, or have you had, a core well-being practice that grows your soil?
- Another way to think of well-being practices are as a form of deep watering. Do you feel your deepest roots (including your taproot) have the sustenance they need? Do you need a deep watering to reset your ability to grow your soil and plants?
- Are the practices you categorized as well-being practices temporary, transactional, transitional, or transformational? What would it take for you to move from temporary all the way to transformational? If you don't already categorize your practice as transformational, is this because of lack of time to dedicate to the practice or lack of regularity? Or is this not the right well-being practice for you?

- Map your obstacles: make a list of internal obstacles and external obstacles. Which ones are truly under your control? Which ones feel insurmountable, even if they are under your control? Can you come up with strategies to address the smallest obstacles first and then move on to the bigger ones? Can you set a timeline for establishing a deep-watering well-being practice?
- It may help to think about some of the things you do automatically (or without much thought), like brushing your teeth.

CHAPTER 9

Awareness

Cotyledon bed,
soft and delicate,
so full of potential.
Miniature canopy,
silky to the touch,
no mistaking
a collective drive.
A purpose
to grow.
Germination rate: 98 percent.
Yet in this abundance,
I am called to thin
more than half.
Play God
with the vulnerable,
who have not yet
set down the roots
to put up a fight.
Each pluck
and gentle tug,
a mistake
in planning
and imagination.

If for better spacing,
there would be less need
for thinning.
What use is
remarkable germination,
if I am not prepared for
its realization?
So much easier
to live in the fantasy of
potential
than
fulfillment.
When I know 98 percent,
why must I create the need
to thin the crop?
Planned abundance
yields double the harvest.

The soil-building approach to leadership is fundamentally about expanding your awareness. Soil of Leadership tools help leaders deepen their ability to perceive and understand themselves, their organizations, and their fields of possibility.

While it is true that leadership is inherently external facing, it is performed and expressed with an emphasis on "how to be" and "what to do." Effective leadership is not possible without attention to the internal core, the taproot, of leadership: who you are.

THE IMPACT OF INTENT

Each of us knows a colleague or leader who strives to learn new skills and techniques and to become more effective (and efficient) practitioners of management and leadership, but they are all performance—an empty suit. Without attention to the foundational elements of what constitutes you, accumulating these skills and credentials is like aimlessly grafting cultivars onto a tree trunk: if the rootstock is mismatched, unhealthy, or even inhospitable, it is all for naught.

For this reason, I begin with the inquiry: Who are you? Not to point you toward finding a singular, convergent identity, but to open a portal for reflection and discovery that many (or even most) leaders have not had the time or space to explore with honesty and in community.

We do this by first focusing on the gulf that can develop between internal intent (how we want to be) and external impact (how we are experienced).

And for many in positions of influence and authority, unfortunately, this gap is wide.

Without the time and space to explore this gap and its causes, people can easily drift and find their internal compass misaligned with their external actions: performing leadership as it is imagined to best be, rather than practicing a leadership that is more aligned with the authentic self. This can push leaders out of integrity and yield results that are not what they hoped. This can result in everything from staff disaffection and unrest to squandered resources and reputational damage to both the leader and the organization.

How is it, many leaders then wonder, that my intention and my impact became so misaligned? I meant to do good in the world, generate positive outcomes, and leave my mark; instead, my reputation is in tatters and my organization is moribund.

Too often our sense of urgency leads us to focus so tightly on improving impact (plants), that we become narrow-minded or blinkered in our work, looking outward for quick wins or quick fixes, in the form of acquiring new skills and techniques or even connecting to more resources, people, and opportunities.

In fact, the crucial first step to improving impact is to turn inward, to your soil, and build your ability to perceive the relationship between impact and intent.

We all experience misalignments between intent and impact. You say something you intend as a compliment, and someone else takes it as an insult; we build a system intended to create equitable outcomes, but we have left someone out of the consultative process and so our work generates unintended consequences. I'm sure you have your own examples, large and small.

No one is free from misalignment, and these moments are often very hard on everyone involved. When individuals find that their intentions do not have the expected impact, they can retreat into their personal perspectives and disconnect from the way(s) they are experienced by others, making excuses, or even feel like the victim, regardless of whether they have hurt another.

The task of a leader is to take responsibility for shaping and shifting the culture and perspectives that lead to misalignment, and in order to do that, leaders must learn how to see that each misalignment is a ripe opportunity for learning, discovery, and connection.

Earlier in the book, we explored how reflection and inquiry can slow down the action and, again, carve out a pathway for new ways of looking at things.

A first step in building toward alignment is to take the time to develop a relationship of awareness with your intent by inserting inquiry into the picture:

Intent (I will) ⟶ Impact (I do)
Intent (I will) ⟶ Inquiry (I wonder) ⟶ Impact (I do)

This far into *The Soil of Leadership*, you already know about the power of inquiry and reflection and how they shift time and create space for you to go deeper and get closer to the root of the matter.

What does inquiry add in this case?

Before you can align impact and intent, you must be sure that you really understand the impact you seek to have. To understand this better, let's zoom into something every leader has to wrestle with: office politics and intergroup relations.

Have you ever had a colleague who thinks he is always helping others, but in fact is regularly undermining their authority by stepping in where his "help" is not needed? Or a boss who thinks they are developing staff capacity, but in fact is micromanaging and telling everyone exactly how to execute every step of every task? Imagine asking that person in your mind: "What was your intention?" To help! To make the work go faster! To teach a junior colleague how to do a task correctly!

Now, ask yourself how it feels to be on the receiving end of any of those interventions. My experience indicates that some of your responses might be diminished, humiliated, frustrated, irritated, condescended to, or even manipulated. If that colleague or boss stopped to ask themselves, "What am I trying to accomplish by helping?" and answered honestly, they might have found something closer to: "I am actually trying to assert my own authority" or "I need to be in control."

Inserting honest, self-focused inquiry into the intention ⟷ impact loop is essential to stopping yourself from engaging (intentionally or unintentionally) in organization- and trust-destroying behaviors. It is how you bridge the gulf between intention and impact, bring yourself into greater self-awareness, better alignment, and more effective and authentic leadership practice.

ALL ABOUT THE SOIL

The young person who returned home to California immediately after living on a traditional, sustainable, community-based farm in Japan was not the kind of guest you want at a friendly dinner party. I was in that sweet spot where righteousness, evangelism, and a clear read on the impending apocalypse are propped up by just enough lived experience to make you off-putting to even the most patient of people. I was not the one you wanted to get stuck sitting next to.

So when the opportunity to start my own farm presented itself, just months after coming back, I was clear that I was going to start with the soil, lead with soil, and end with the soil—and no one was going to change that. *Everything* would be about the soil.

A central tenet of good soil management is a sound cropping plan, and so I came into this farm with a very elaborate, three-year crop rotation schedule, fully focused on long-term soil health. The plan was filled with heirloom, open-pollinated varieties of nightshades (tomatoes, peppers, eggplants), chenopods (spinach, chard), and brassicas (broccoli, cabbage, cauliflower), and featured other items such as purple amaranth, endive, and radicchio. According to my calculations, I would have a thriving community of pollinators—honeybees and monarch butterflies—to ensure the growth of nutrient-dense vegetables within soil so precious it would feel at home atop a pedestal. I was even more certain than I had been on my first clumsy day in Japan that I had all the right answers.

My spreadsheet was going to recreate the Garden of Eden.

It could be said that successful farming is as much about timing and readiness as anything else. Plant too early and watch a late season cold snap freeze it out; wait a few days too long and suffer a field overrun by weeds. Sustainable farmers know that to be successful, they have to take multiple factors into consideration before putting a plant or seed into the ground, as the very act sets in motion a chain of events that require significant time, resources, labor, and work. For this reason, they ask themselves questions like: Is this the right variety to be planting? Is this the right timing? Are the conditions conducive and ready to support this planting? These are important inquiries that grow the awareness for how to more closely align intent (a successful planting) and impact (a successful harvest).

My experience is that leaders can learn a lot from this discernment process, particularly in how it explores and fundamentally depends on the relationship between intention and impact.

RECREATING THE FARM

"Um, so how are you planning to sell that amaranth?"

This was from my farming partner, the one who was financially supporting my farming endeavor. Like me, a Japanese American, he was about a half generation older than me, and our families knew each other in the ways that people do in immigrant communities: my grandmother was his family's childhood dentist. His family had continued their work in agriculture, and he had become a very successful conventional farmer (and later the California Secretary of Agriculture), specializing in celery, cabbage, and strawberries. When he heard that I had been living in Japan and practicing sustainable farming, he reached out and proposed a partnership on six acres of land that sat between two housing tracts. Full of ideas (and myself), I jumped right in.

Fortunately, farming, like leadership, is an inherently humbling practice. Or at least it was for me. After just a few weeks into my time on that farm, his question about amaranth exposed the gap between my righteous rhetoric of intent and the growing reality of likely impact. For all that I had learned and done, my life on the Japanese farm did not require me to wrestle with a few essential things: How am I going to make a living? What happens if there is a pest infestation? Who possibly wants to buy my purple amaranth?

When I was dreaming up my spreadsheets, I assumed my farm would be like Dr. Takekuma's: whatever production comes out of the soil will find its way to a very happy consumer. It was clear to me that we would be selling in farmers' markets and via other farm-to-consumer strategies, like Community Supported Agriculture (CSA), but I had not considered how Dr. Takekuma could plant *and* sell such a diverse bounty of crops—some of which were not the typical vegetables that would fly off the shelves of Japanese supermarkets. It went beyond his success in cultivating the conditions for growth on the farm itself, the literal soil.

Dr. Takekuma's farm wasn't just a farm—far beyond the CSA and farmers' market offerings, it was the beating heart of an extended community. He had thoughtfully built a larger ecosystem that consisted of a wide-ranging network of community-based groups that would bus their members to a hospital where groups of ten to five hundred people would get their annual health checkups and learn about health issues—such as the benefits of the traditional Japanese diet for staving off chronic conditions—delivered in the local dialect by Dr. Takekuma. They then would be bused over to the farm for a traditional Japanese meal, sourced from our farm and supplemented by food items from local farming partners.

One couple stands out to me particularly, for the multifaceted way in which the relationship manifested itself. They were from a nearby former mining town, so much like all the other places where narrowly focused business interests enter, extract, and get out—and leave behind all kinds of fallout, including poisons that lead to negative health outcomes for local residents. Despite being only forty-five, the husband had developed significant kidney problems, and in response, they had found Dr. Takekuma's community. To help the husband's recovery, the couple was committed to eating food grown in our soil. As part of that commitment, they would come to community days or drop by unannounced and help weed for an hour on their way to the farmers' market and then the pharmacy. You could see in their daily practice how their connection to this farm supported their well-being. It was not just a place, but a community of deep engagement. They came not only to eat the farm's output, but to be part of the input, tending the field, buying the produce, returning their organic scraps to the compost pile.

They participated in every stage in the life cycle of that food and of the community that grew it.

A creative, entrepreneurial enterprise, Dr. Takekuma's farm vastly expanded my ideas about what a farm could do and what role it plays in social, as well as biological, systems, education, and health. He had his community partners—rice and dairy farmers—who would contribute to the meals; he had ten thousand people coming to his farm each year. He also had an annual community of dozens of work-study farm workers, of which I was one—a group of young people, mostly Japanese, who came to the farm seeking something, as I had, and who invariably left with the same addiction to building community.

Even though I had seen all of this "above ground," it took me struggling to replicate my learning on my own farm in California to realize the reason for Dr. Takekuma's success was his ability to cultivate the larger context and interconnectedness that supported the farm economically but also sustained it as an interdependent community: creating a place where people felt trusted, supported, and thus, empowered to try their hand at planting their most audacious ideas. That was the context in which his farm thrived. That was *his* soil. He had taught me, and so many others, to grow there. His community was the soil in which I truly began rooting my sense of purpose: I saw and lived things that inspired me to want to recreate that in the United States.

I had the farm, but I had yet to cultivate the conditions. I had the clear intent, but it was nowhere near where it needed to be to achieve significant impact—or at least the kind of impact that would enable me to farm season after season.

If I didn't get into a different mindset, I wouldn't be farming very long. Yes, I needed to grow soil, but I also needed to plant things that people would pay money for—and relatively soon. I couldn't just print out a recipe and hope thousands of customers would line up to pay out the money I needed to recoup the costs of growing my favorite superfood.

This was not a hobby. This was not for charity. This was work.

My intentions were not enough.

SELF-AWARENESS

Self-awareness is a tricky task. For as much as we would all like to think that we are capable of clearly and honestly assessing our inner states of being, the reality is that our self-perceptions can be greatly distorted and lead to disconnection from our surroundings. At the same time, it is critical in leadership that we each have some capacity to check in with ourselves and articulate what is going on.

And while there are countless nuanced and robust frameworks for making such determinations, as leaders we typically do not have the time nor space to undergo such analysis. For this reason, I want to offer a simple way to assess your state of being: expansion and contraction.

Expansion is the realm of possibility and exploration. It is when you are creative, divergent, adaptive, and connected to learning new things. When we are in a state of expansion, there is a certain kind of openness where we invite transformation.

Contraction is the realm of certainty and determination. It is when you are conservative, convergent, firm, and connected to your existing beliefs. When we are in a state of contraction, there is a certain kind of defensiveness where we are closed to new inputs.

But let me be clear—while it may seem the case, there is nothing inherently good or bad about either. Furthermore, both states of being are necessary. At any given moment we may swing from being in expansion to in contraction.

For our purposes, what is important are the answers to two questions:

- Are you currently in a state of expansion or contraction?
- Is this where you want to be?

And even more important than your answer to the first question is your answer to the second: Is this where you want to be?

Because if the answer is "no," then you have some work to do.

WAIT—Why Am I Talking?

We have all found ourselves at times when the moment called for better listening and we filled it with louder talking. For many of us, sitting in silence or letting others lead a meeting can be challenging. WAIT stands for Why Am I Talking? This gentle self-awareness tool can remind us of the importance of listening and observing over talking and asserting. In fact, if you WAIT, you may well find that your team or colleagues can solve a problem more effectively than if you jumped in and told them how *you* would solve it. If you find that you often struggle with WAITing, consider these questions:

- Are my words generative (adding) or degenerative (diminishing) contributions to the conversation and to others' ability to learn, grow, or work effectively together?
- Is there a question I can ask to keep me in a state of inquiry rather than judgment?
- How are my words preventing other viewpoints, perspectives, and/or voices from contributing?

A VIABLE BEAN FARM

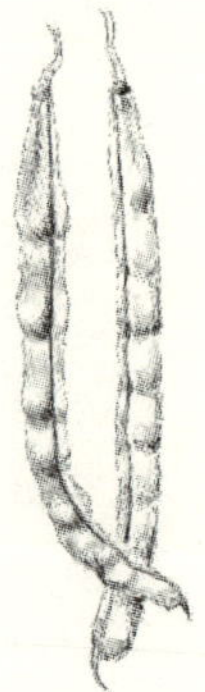

"Well, maybe instead of amaranth, there's something else that can be grown?"

My partner had posed a reasonable question, given that I had no real idea who would be excited to pay money (never mind eat) my purple amaranth.

"Our farm has a lot of experience with fresh green beans. They grow fast and well in this climate, and the broker that sells our conventional beans said that organic beans can fetch a significant premium as long as there's enough to sell. So maybe to start, we plant the entire field to beans?"

My righteous indignation rose up. Ugh. Not even a full month into the work of nurturing a truly sustainable, biodiverse farm, I was being presented with an offer to monocrop. But at the same time, I was quickly becoming aware that no one wanted my purple amaranth—and that was not the compost pile I wanted to die on.

So I agreed, and the first thing I did as a sustainable farmer was give over five of my six acres to beans. It was not the farm in Japan. It didn't look like the farm I had imagined, with its riot of color and biodiversity. But we planted, we harvested, and we sold it. Revenue came in—not a lot, but it was something. We put it in crates, gave it to a wholesaler, and that was the end of it. No happy consumer with a farmers' market basket over their arm and a dream of a Saturday evening farm-to-table feast in their heart. We were lucky to get a nod and a wave from the flatbed driver as he pulled off the farm with crates in tow.

It was a clarifying experience to produce a commodity for the chain, after the gut punch of letting go of the thinking, "I can grow a six-acre garden," and recognizing, "What I need to do is produce a viable business. And if I don't do that, I will no longer be in business."

The conventional farmer I was in partnership with liked to say that he was a sustainable farmer because, at the end of season, he had enough money to plant a crop for the next cycle. Not in the spirit of the term, to be sure, but in terms of economics, he was right.

I had to ask myself: "If I want to farm as a business, I have to reshape my approach. What does that look like, and is it too different from what I set out to do?"

These are questions for anyone who is drawn to work infused with idealism: What does someone with clarity of purpose do when they find themselves in a system they do not want to actively be a part of? Burn it all down, drop out, and live in a strawbale house as a barefoot gardener?

I was struggling at the intersection of expansion and contraction.

So I planted the beans.

But no sooner had the tears dried on the spreadsheet, than I was able to appreciate I hadn't let all my principles wither on the vine: by coating the seeds in an inoculant, I was able to use them to fix the nitrogen in the soil, which meant that I was both getting the short-term harvest to bring to market *and* the long-term goal of soil building. Plant-based *and* soil-based.

If I were coaching the younger me through this decision of whether to give up on my spreadsheets of amaranth and endive, I would first ask the question: "What are you trying to do and why?" followed by, "Based on the limited information that you are currently working with, does this decision help to bring you closer to realizing that sense of purpose?"

In the case of the green beans, the answer was "yes."

Had he proposed to me fumigating the field with methyl bromide and planting strawberries to make some quick money before we got the clock started on the organic certification process, the answer would have certainly been "no."

But by the same token, had I clung to my amaranth dreams and started the first year deep in debt, I would have been equally distant from my purpose to build and renew community through a farming that prioritizes connection.

My partnership with the conventional farmer also did something very important.

It taught me that intent cannot be divorced from an honest engagement with impact.

And perhaps even more importantly, it taught a self-awareness that reminded me that my purpose was not about striving to always be in a state of expansion (what this farm could be) and/or contraction (my righteousness), but rather how I could best adapt and (re)align my clear purpose to the changing circumstances.

Self-Awareness and Leading Human Rights Advocacy in Iraq

"In my journey as a geopolitical researcher and journalist focusing on Iraq and northeast Syria, I have discovered the transformative power of self-awareness and its impact on my advocacy work. My primary goal is to shed light on the intricate political dynamics, human rights challenges, and geopolitical complexities faced by the people in these regions. However, I have come to realize that good intentions alone are insufficient. It is crucial to bridge the gap between intention and impact through self-reflection and evaluation. By cultivating self-awareness, I have recognized the potential for unintended consequences in my advocacy efforts. While my intention is to highlight human rights abuses and amplify the voices of marginalized communities, I now understand the importance of considering alternative narratives and perspectives. This awareness has compelled me to continually reflect on my work, question my assumptions, and inquire honestly into the outcomes and effects of my efforts. By embracing this approach, I have been able to enhance my leadership practice and become more effective and authentic in my advocacy. It has enabled me to develop a mindful understanding of the complexities of the region, challenge my own biases, and contribute to a more comprehensive and inclusive comprehension of the geopolitical landscape. Motivated by my love for the people I aim to serve, I have embraced discipline and a sense of responsibility. These qualities have pushed me to push beyond the boundaries of my comfort zone and consistently strive for growth and improvement. I believe that true leadership lies in acknowledging the impact of our actions and taking responsibility for their consequences. By doing so, we can foster positive change and contribute to a better future for those we care about."

Mustafa Hasan (Iraq)
Journalist
International Centre for Counter-Terrorism

Awareness Building in Burundi

"Building awareness has been instrumental in my work as a social entrepreneur in Burundi. When working with individuals from highly vulnerable backgrounds, we recognize the importance of tailoring our approaches to address their specific challenges and aspirations. Through ongoing dialogue, active listening, and cultural sensitivity, we have feedback mechanisms to promote a greater understanding of their needs and desires. But it starts with paying attention to my self-awareness and understanding who I am at my core. This requires introspection, reflection, and an honest exploration of my intentions and their impact on others. It's not easy work, but the payoff is worth it."

Ange Muco Muyubira (Burundi)
Founder & Executive Director
Kaz'O'zah Art

REFLECTION

As you complete this chapter, I invite you to take a moment to pause and reflect on the following inquiries.

- Every leader has tried to grow plants without tending to the soil. Are you consciously growing soil or plants? It is okay to acknowledge to yourself that you are growing plants and, perhaps, that you have neglected the soil. But if you now see that you are largely (or solely) plant focused, take some time to reflect on whether this is through your own deliberate actions or whether you are puzzled about how you came to allocate your time and energy this way.
- Now, whether you assess that you are growing plants, or soil, or both, ask yourself if you are currently in a state of expansion or contraction?
- If you are currently in a state of contraction, how is that serving your organization? Are you contracting out of fear, are you overwhelmed, or are you contracting without having yet reflected on why or how you came to be in this state?
- If you are in a state of expansion, write down three new things you want to know or do in order to push your field of vision out further.

- I don't always recommend looking to other leaders for inspiration, but are there people in your life (leaders or not) that you consider to be very self-aware? What is it about their behavior and/or being that leads you to believe this? Would it encourage you into a state of expansion to adopt (or at least try on) some of their practices, behaviors, and orientations? To try on some of the practices (e.g., WAIT) presented in this book?
- Is there a time when you "planted the beans"? When you look back on that decision, what would you tell your younger self? Can you take that advice now?

CHAPTER 10

Working Together

In it together
to save the world
shouldn't end
with
an email.

My love of soil proved no mere infatuation: the enormity of life in but one handful of earth, the smell of transformation, it was unlike anything I had ever experienced. But as much as I enjoyed the production aspects of farming, my experience on Dr. Takekuma's farm brought my true purpose into sharp relief: community development and social impact *through* agricultural practice—not farming with a side of education. Witnessing how people would change, just by visiting and working on the farm for a few days, was something to behold: using their bodies as intended and feeling all senses.

So when it came time for me to start my own farm, much of what we did was about education. For every conversation about cropping plans, there were three more about how to bring more people from the surrounding Southern California community onto the land to put their hands into the soil. My partnership with the large-scale conventional farmer was just a stepping stone to help me get my bearings on the way to my ultimate vision: an educational farm where people could congregate to learn, eat, and connect. A farm where people could stay and experience something meaningful, with the ultimate goal that they would establish a closer relationship to themselves, one another, and the natural world.

This place was to be called Coastal Sage Farms.

COASTAL SAGE FARMS

Named after the native plant community in which it was to be situated, I envisioned Coastal Sage Farms as a place where I would fully express my professional purpose as well as the literal soil on which I would experience so many of the passages of life. To help realize this vision, a group of four core partners was assembled—myself, my best friend with whom I was farming at the time, an organic farmer from the area, and another friend who would provide the capital to purchase the land.

In the cracks of downtime on the farm, we created a detailed business plan, began to map out roles and responsibilities, and investigated several pieces of land throughout Central and Southern California. It was a passionate vision fueled by a strong sense of righteousness and shared purpose—the four of us were aligned on an endeavor that was not only going to provide us with a right livelihood; it was going to save the world. While we had created a business plan, we waved away other formalities, like written agreements, since we were bonded under a higher purpose.

It was a partnership around a sense of a shared destiny. We were all in it together. It was ideal.

That is, until it wasn't.

After Coastal Sage Farms folded, I remember conducting a psychological postmortem of blame, focused on the individual personalities and assigning fault as to why things didn't work out. *That person lacked commitment. The other person didn't understand responsibility.* Indicative of my poor self-awareness and unrefined ego, I quickly moved to blame others for their lack of purposeful partnership. The options were: either we were working together, or we were not. And after several months I concluded: we were not.

What I did not realize is that collaborations, especially those that aim for the stars, cannot thrive on goodwill alone. Nor can they be summed up in an either/or frame: either we are collaborating, or we are not.

It would only be years later that I understood that the answers to why this collaboration failed were, in fact, all around me on the farm—we had not cultivated the conditions for a partnership so weighty with intention to be able to grow and flourish. Our intention to build a working residential farm that would generate immediate output (income) and leave a long-term impact (legacy) meant that we needed deep roots and careful planning at every stage to ensure sustainability.

I lacked the language to name and articulate collaboration in a richer and more refined way and, as a result, was unable to recognize that even the most inspired and purposeful partnerships—perhaps these most of all—need to have transactional and formalized aspects.

While we each knew the nuts and bolts of what we were individually bringing to the partnership (for three of us, farming knowledge and community ties; for one of us, money), we never had any kind of meaningful conversation about the implications of those diverse contributions. Nor did we ever collectively explore what each of us were hoping to get out of the partnership.

With no real sense of the gaps in our assumptions, fissures were sure to emerge, but we were not prepared. It was a collaboration powered by high-minded rhetoric that pushed us to soar to new heights, but we failed, leaving a fragile construct exposed on the ground beneath us. Put differently, it was all flowers and fruits, no roots.

So after six years of centering agriculture in my life and with a shattered vision at my feet, I found myself at a crossroads. Without the excitement of building toward an educational farm, my motivation waned. It was becoming clearer to me that the circumstances—the conditions—in which I was doing my work were not aligned with my purpose to build and renew community through a farming that prioritized connection. More and more, I found myself overwhelmed by the kinds of things that come at you when building a new business, without the spoonful of sugar to make it palatable. The gravity of busyness pulled me toward a state in which I felt overworked, underpaid, and increasingly adrift from why I had set out to do all this in the first place. My hope and optimism had been replaced by cynicism and bitterness.

I needed change.

Before I led a life in agriculture, I had wanted to pursue a doctoral degree. I had some romantic sense of what that would mean—quiet hours in libraries filled with filtered light, the space to explore ideas, and eventually a position that would provide full license to wear a tweed jacket with elbow patches without a hint of irony. So after six years of being a full-time farmer, I did what many do when we don't know where to turn, but we don't want to have to explain ourselves to family and friends.

I went to graduate school.

ACADEMIC LIFE AND LANGUAGE

Not surprisingly, I entered academic life with an arrogance that rivaled my first return to the United States from Dr. Takekuma's farm. In this case, high on years of practical work experience (or so I felt at the time) and the real struggle to make a positive impact in the world, I didn't start my studies with what one might call an "open learning posture." In fact, I was regularly in a state of contraction, as although I was certain that I needed another credential to realize my long-term visions, I was equally skeptical that I would learn anything of real value in an academic environment. I wanted in and out, so that I could get on with my life.

What I would quickly learn, however, just a few weeks into my first quarter, was that being back in school and exposure to academic frameworks was helping me to see the past six years of farming in a deeper, more meaningful light. As I was placed in a more expansive state of mind, acquiring language that would help me better understand how my specific pursuits were shaped by systemic forces of political economy and social constructs, I was able to see how it was not the work of farming that animated my passions, but the way that connecting people to living soil brought me (and them) joy. Being back in school helped me to see that, for me, connecting people to living soil had little to do with agriculture and everything to do with learning—namely, how learning could transform people's lives for the better.

Going back to school provided me with an opportunity to get at the roots of things and, most importantly, with the language to be able to name and articulate so many of the experiences that I had previously lacked the words to describe. It moved me from talking about my work as "building and renewing community through an *agriculture* that prioritizes connection" to focusing on "building and renewing community through *learning* that prioritizes connection."

To experience this intellectual evolution was exhilarating, and it opened up an entirely new way of looking at and being in the world.

And yet I had traded one set of challenges and frustrations and expressions of ego for another. The animating insights I was experiencing in my graduate studies were inextricable from the deeply rooted norms of individualism and competition required to survive and thrive in the academic context—to say nothing of the shroud of opaque language cocooning each concept, terms like social construction, positionality, cultural hegemony and doxa.

How was I going to translate this outside the ivory tower?

I struggled with the impracticality of a life of the mind and, even more so, with just how poorly (shockingly so) people in academic contexts work with others. Rare is the graduate student or junior faculty member who lacks a see-it-to-believe-it story of mean-spirited territorialism, wild temper tantrums, rude public critiques, or self-aggrandizing behavior wildly out of step with acceptable social norms.

You could say that graduate school offered me a field guide about all the ways that collaboration can fail.

But even as the potential for collaboration in an academic setting faded into the distance, my years in graduate school gave me language to articulate the socially constructed nature of reality, and it also gave me the imperative to translate these ideas into more accessible language. A language that articulates a clear, actionable practice of making meaning with others, tweed jacket not required.

Collaborative partnerships are often animated by the question "Should we?" An affirmative on both sides ends all preliminaries, and it's off to the races. Absolutely, let's collaborate.

However, as I learned in the early, rocky phase of my time working in startups, the true preface to collaboration needs to be: "What do we mean by collaboration, are we able to do what is necessary to achieve it, and is our context able to support it?" Put differently, "Is now the time, is here the place, and are we the people?"

WORKING TOGETHER TO ACHIEVE SOMETHING

From the Latin "to work together," collaboration implies we work together, not simply in parallel, to achieve a common purpose. We draw on one another's distinct talents, experiences, visions, and resources in order to get something done that we couldn't do on our own. A lyricist and a composer collaborate on a song. An architect and a contractor collaborate on a house. The marketing and research departments collaborate on a presentation. Two organizations collaborate to cross-promote an initiative to their respective audiences.

Long-term or short, lofty or banal, collaboration is capacious enough to entertain all manners of working together. Yet if collaboration is working together *to achieve something,* it must start with parameters.

If we scattered a random packet of seeds in a patch of earth at a random time of year and then tended to them according to our whim, the chances anything would germinate would be rather slight—let alone that it would grow into the thing we want it to be.

When we start a collaboration, in farming terms, we have to know what we are planting and why. From there, we can consider the conditions required to help it thrive and whether we are able to meet them; we can plan for contingencies and inevitable curveballs; we can think long term about how a collaboration may sustain itself or, if it runs its course, peaceably end.

Each collaboration will be unique—and no schema could hope to cover all scenarios.

That said, I have built the following model through years of practice, informed by theory, reshaped by more practice, and then tweaked with another dose of theory. My understanding of collaboration comes from personal experiences—on the farm, in academia, and in the world of business—enriched, complicated, and augmented by my experiences supporting leaders of all stages in their collaborations.

Central to my philosophy on collaboration is that there is no hierarchy of collaborative types. There isn't a "better" level, and the goal isn't necessarily to go deeper in every collaboration. The measure of the strength of a collaboration is the extent to which the rhetoric and reality align—not the extent to which the partners tout a transformational sense of a shared destiny. As I elaborate below, purely transactional collaborations not only can be *good,* but they are the core of what it means to work with others in a more equitable and inclusive way. Not all relationships have the conditions (soil) to support a transformational collaboration. In fact, as was the case with Coastal Sage Farms, most do not.

I introduce the model with a goal of naming what is there—building awareness—so that we know where we are in our collaborations and what we can expect to give and to receive, keeping in mind that relationships and collaborations regularly move in and out of different realms and can be in more than one at the same time.

Exchanging Resources

Spectrum of Collaboration

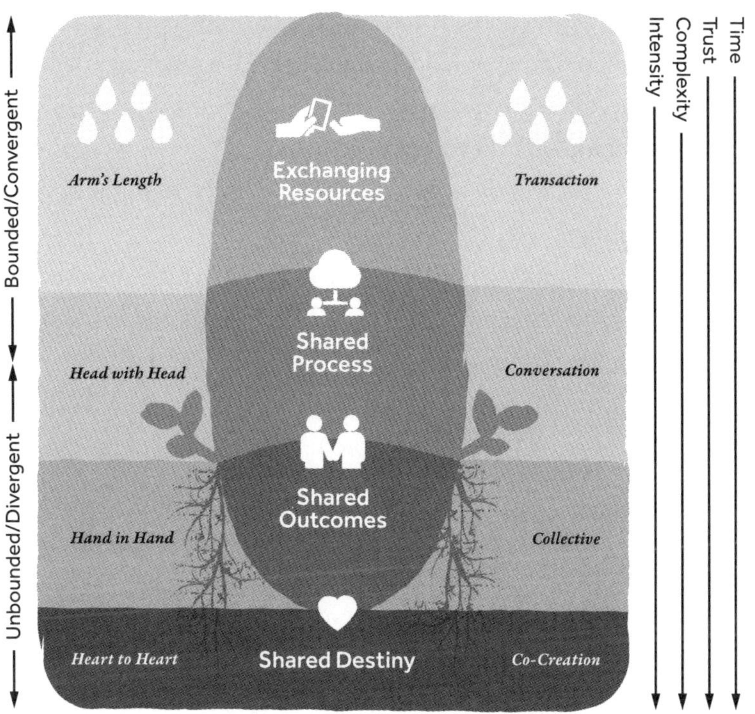

Starting from the top, there is Exchanging Resources. This is collaboration at its most basic. Working in this sphere can mean trading skills or pooling efforts—two heads are better than one, and four hands more efficient than two—in the interest of a common purpose. The emotional distance between the parties tends to be at arm's length, largely because the terms of the transaction are bound and converge around a particular set or sets of outcomes.

For example, say two neighbors decide to come together to plant a garden. One has a sunny plot of land with deer-proof fencing and a garage full of tools. The other has years of experience on their childhood farm and plenty of free time. Each has something the other one needs in order to get what both want: fresh produce.

Together, they fill the beds with all their favorites, deciding how to divide up chores, expenses, and, eventually, the harvest. Come winter, each retreats to their respective home, and at the first signs of spring, they decide whether they want to try again. A poor harvest or the moment one secures their own plot of land likely spells the end of the relationship.

From a soil-building perspective, this realm is plant-focused—interested in outputs and outcomes. While it may seem like a simple relationship that is not animated by passion and/or deep commitment, it still requires time and trust between parties for it to continue successfully—as well as external structure, such as formal governing agreements, especially in the early days. Values and purpose may stimulate the relationship, and while the roots may not run deep, they are there, nevertheless.

A collaboration that tries to grow beyond this realm without putting in the work will be fragile at its core.

Some questions to ask to help you locate yourself in this layer:

- Are the terms of the collaboration easy to define? Who's getting what, where, how, when, and why?
- Is there a clear time frame and/or end point?
- Are the boundaries for the terms of the collaboration clearly defined and/or not intended to be breached?

Shared Process

As we move deeper into the soil and expand out to cover a broader swath of land, the second sphere, Shared Process, indicates a subtle but important opening up, where the parties are involved in an ongoing conversation, rendering the partnership less fixed and bounded and more open to change and adaptation.

In the case of our neighborhood garden, a Shared Process collaboration would show up in different ways. Instead of just providing resources to one another and retreating to their respective homes, the neighbors learn from one another while they work side by side, sharing knowledge and stories.

When an issue arises, like a pest infestation, there's no moment of crisis, and when there's an unexpectedly bountiful yield, the two partners look to one another to decide how to handle it: do they want to donate it, hold a neighborhood banquet, or gorge themselves on infinite carrots? Maybe they want to let some go to seed, investing in the future of their partnership, allowing the carrot flowers to attract beneficial insects—and provide heirloom seeds two years later. It's not just about the carrots they eat today but the garden they'll tend tomorrow. How then does this process of negotiation inform the potential pathway to collaboration?

The intended outcomes are a strong part of the structure, but the space for conversation means that the collaboration evolves and grows beyond just transaction. In our language, we're shifting to include more of a soil-based orientation to balance the heavily plant-based approach. Of course, in order to have these kinds of meaningful conversations, the parties must spend more time together and develop a higher degree of trust. And as is the case when people come closer together, their relationship takes on a greater complexity and intensity. This kind of collaboration requires devoting more time and attention to building an open understanding of the purposes and roles within the collaboration. And while the root system is growing, the collaboration may not yet be able or ready to withstand high demands and change. It is, therefore, important to not make assumptions about the strength of the foundation.

Some questions to ask to help you to locate yourself in this layer:

- Is there a spirit of conversation and/or exploration in the collaboration?
- Is there an openness to change, depending on how things evolve?
- How would you handle an unexpected event and/or challenge?

Shared Outcomes

Continuing our probing into deeper layers of the soil and the broadest swath of land, we now come to the sphere of Shared Outcomes.

The big shift here is from a sense of how things work separately for the different parties involved in the collaboration to how the collaboration offers a collective benefit. This shift from me/you to us/we is simple in rhetoric but difficult in reality. As it implies, this level of collaboration requires a deeper consideration from all parties about what it means to create a "we," and therefore, issues related to such things as power differentials, inherited wealth and privilege, and unconscious bias and exclusion need to be acknowledged and addressed.

Now consider the neighborhood garden in this collective realm. This isn't just a space where strangers plant and harvest seasonal vegetables in physical proximity. Weekly work sessions turn into a time to talk of what goes beyond the salad greens: perennial plants that will take longer to establish themselves but promise to provide a long-term yield and stability to the space; a community gathering place that extends the garden's radius beyond the outer fence.

As each neighbor shows up, does the work, and shares themselves, their individual interests and needs can come together to serve a shared purpose, and their shared trust can move them on beyond the world of dreams.

Now, as they harvest their seasonal crops, they are also shifting toward new priorities—identifying how the garden can accommodate learning experiences. The garden is well-established enough that it does not need constant tending. The intention behind it allows them to look beyond the daily chores and think about what else can grow there.

When they run across obstacles and disagreements, the regular dialogue and the shared purpose provide the resilience to engage and withstand. A single storm won't wipe it out. A poor yield of a crop will not be catastrophic.

In this realm, we can find a balance between plant- and soil-based orientation, shifting focus between short- and long-term goals as needed. Yes, there will be output—but the fruits of their collective labor will be both tangible and intangible.

Anyone who has undertaken this kind of intense work knows that it requires a great deal of time and trust to successfully navigate, and it inherently leads to a greater richness of complexity within relationships. This work is very often expansive and divergent, as collaborative parties recognize that it is primarily about the connection and the process they undertake together, more than predetermined outcomes. This hand-in-hand work is not easy but serves as the foundation for advancing empathy and transformation within group and organizational life. When done well, it allows for a truly sustainable collaboration that nourishes rather than depletes.

Some questions to ask to help you locate yourself in this layer:

- Do you and your collaborator(s) have a history of working together and building trust?
- Do you and your collaborator(s) have a history of working through challenging situations together and coming out of those situations with a strong connection?
- Have you explored the way(s) that power shapes this collaboration?

Whatever kind of garden you plan, once the seed of collaboration is sown, you have to be sensitive to where each plant is in its growth cycle; you can't expect apples from a year-old sapling, but you can pick tomatoes off a two-month-old vine. No one grows a collective partnership in a day.

By the same token, some collaborations have expiration dates: leave a zucchini on the vine too long, and you'll get a monster veggie that everyone wants to make jokes about—and no one wants to eat.

In some cases, the collaboration you've sown offers you room to make decisions: you can harvest a root crop in one season and eat a carrot, or you can let it become an annual and yield hundreds of carrot seeds for future plantings. Your choice will depend on the parameters you have established: Why did you plant the carrot in the first place? Has the context shifted to change your perspective on that question in the meantime? Are you growing annuals or perennials—and why?

No partnership springs forth from a seed on day one; such is the realm of magic beanstalks (no spoilers required). However, if you start a collaboration and everything seems to be humming away at top speed, give yourself the time and space (and don't say you can't afford it—you can't afford not to) to connect with the soil and perceive what you can.

Ask yourself: have we cultivated the conditions?

If the soil is too compacted for you to get past the topmost layer (does it still seem like just dirt?), you owe it to yourself and to your collaborators to do the kind of work that will allow what you plant to flourish.

A word to the wise: if you think you can skip the work because you and your collaborators are "in this together," to me, that's the strongest indicator of all that there's a need to slow down and dig in.

This work is not easy. Examining and describing the terms of any human-to-human relationship can feel awkward or uncomfortable. What if your partner does not share the same assumptions or ideas about collaboration? If you are misaligned, will that destroy your bond? Well, it might, but that misalignment will likely degrade, if not destroy, your shared enterprise sooner or later, and if it is later, the fallout may be greater than if you had built your shared awareness with intention at an earlier stage, built a shared soil that enabled you each to ask questions like "When will there be pickles?"

Over the years I have often weighed whether to include a fourth layer, Shared Purpose and Destiny ("We are in this together"). Too often I see collaborations fail because the participants *assume* they are aligned toward a shared purpose *and* destiny. For most collaborations, clear, shared purpose is sufficient—shared destiny is not required. Yet so many of us aspire to the truly deep work of cocreation where collaborators are invested in connection at the deepest realm of heart and purpose. This kind of work requires not only a sense of magic, but it also takes dedication and intense commitments of time, space, and trust.

In whatever ways that Shared Outcomes calls upon more time, space, trust, complexity, and intensity from the collaborators, Shared Purpose and Destiny requires that much more. In this realm there is no space for opting out—at least not without significant repercussions. The integration of hearts—the unifying of the separate pieces to create a greater sense of wholeness—this is the realm of love. And as is the case with love, it summons us to meet its highest calling.

To be and remain in this space—especially in organizational and group life—is rare and often fleeting. And yet this does not stop the rhetoric of shared purpose and destiny from being spread around as though it can take root everywhere.

COLLABORATION RHETORIC

As anyone who has worked in the social sector knows, it is common for the organizational mission and vision to be invoked as inspirational drives to action and a call for staff members to put the work of the organization over their personal needs. While effective in moving people to action in resource-limited contexts, this approach can also result in a culture of martyrdom, where boundaries blur and things like compensation and clarity of role are sidelined. It is not uncommon to hear people (often with a sense of pride) talk about putting their heart and soul into the work and to hear the language of "family" and "us versus them" used to describe the workplace.

I have a vivid memory of introducing this partnership model to a group of leaders from East Africa. All were highly accomplished and successful, and many worked for mission-driven organizations that were focused on doing things like ending poverty, empowering women and girls, or providing safety and stability for vulnerable populations.

Without question important work—the kind that puts significant demands on one's time and energy.

After presenting the model, a participant with prominent gray in their hair raised their hand and said, "For the last ten years I believed that I was working together with my board in heart-to-heart, shared destiny and purpose, but I was just told that they are going to replace me, even though I am the founder. I gave over so much of my life to building this organization, giving up opportunities to make more money and have more prestige, and now I am being pushed out with very little to take forward. As it is a nonprofit organization, I do not have any ownership rights and, really, all that I have are the memories of the good work. But good memories don't support old age. I now can see that I should have paid more attention to the transactional pieces of my connection to the organization. My assumption that we were all family—and you don't fire family—was overly simple-minded."

It was a striking moment of sharing. Not only for the significance of their circumstances, but also for how it brought voice to the ways in which collaboration rhetoric can obscure and be used to exploit partnerships, especially in contexts where people are there for the love of the work. Nonprofits and academia are particularly susceptible to this, but the rhetoric-reality gap is real in all sectors and in all parts of the world.

THE RHETORIC-REALITY GAP

The rhetoric-reality gap often disproportionately hurts the party with less power and fewer resources, but there are reasons for those with the upper hand to pay it heed. Accurately naming and nurturing the desired kinds of collaboration is one way for an organization, team, or partnership to cultivate the conditions. While one might be able to yield a quick harvest out of a disingenuous call to sacrificing for the greater good, that kind of plant-based proposition will never sustain itself over multiple seasons. Eventually, the depleted soil will refuse to bear fruit and the crisis will come to a head.

For many years I have worked closely with an international organization that has nearly half a century of experience serving vulnerable youth throughout Latin America by providing young people who are either unhoused or in precarious domestic configurations with greater access to education, stability, and a community of support. The ongoing work is admirable, and because of their long track record in the region, tens of thousands of people have benefitted from their programs, yielding a deeply loyal community of beneficiaries, many of whom have gone on to become staff.

While this is a great testament to the organization's impact and enduring legacy, it also creates some challenges. There is an implicit expectation that if you work for the organization, you put all of your heart and soul into the work with children, with things like compensation, clarity and boundary of role, and even personal well-being coming in as lesser priorities. Therefore, staff members who are perceived as not buying into this level of commitment are characterized as being "problems." Sometimes, it is even voiced that hiring priorities should be in favor of people who, at one time, were actual beneficiaries of the organization's programs, irrespective of someone's actual qualifications.

So here there is a significant discrepancy between the perception and assumption of what it means to be a collaborating team member and how some team members understand their role, where it is a job first and a lifestyle second. In fact, what this organization has needed for a long time is highly qualified people who are the right people for the work. What has persisted is an approach that places people who are deeply committed to the organization in positions where they are severely underqualified.

In my work with this group, this model has helped to illustrate that there is not anything inherently problematic about having people on staff who are there "just" to get a paycheck. So long as they are doing their work, at a high level, is it really a problem that they were not direct beneficiaries of the organization's programs? And is it really what the organization wants to be doing—consistently managing the complex and intense relationships that require significant amounts of time—when *as an organization* it needs to actually do the work? What's the priority: to provide the services or to provide jobs as one of the services?

This approach to understanding collaboration and purpose is particularly helpful when considering relations with those who hold power and resources. Whereas I once sought out those who speak the language of connection, cocreation, and transformation, now I am wary and skeptical of those who position themselves in these ways, especially in contexts where there has been no investment in cultivating the conditions nor a compelling plan to allow the time and space to grow such deep roots.

Once we have a language for talking about collaboration, we can get more granular and apply it to our specific situation. One way we can do that is with a tool called a Collaboration Screen (visit the Soil of Leadership website to download the tool). This tool pushes you (and others) to answer foundational questions and, by knowing the answers, can help inform decisions on how or if you should enter into a partnership.

The success of this tool will depend on the rigor with which you approach it: answer each question thoroughly. If you find that there are some questions that you cannot answer, that is something to pay attention to.

After doing the qualitative work of answering each question, assign a number to each category. While this is not scientific analysis, it does the important work of assigning a fixed answer to what is often a very nebulous context (working together).

I have used this tool with clients and partners at the individual level, helping leaders to discern and reflect on potential collaborations, and also at the collective level, where a group of people share their thoughts and/or responses to the various questions, thus engaging in a collaborative inquiry to get clearer on the "What's going on here?" question that shapes so much of our life in leadership.

A serious engagement with this tool will go a long way in setting the stage for working together in a relationship that, while not free from disagreements, will have a greater chance of avoiding disconnection.

POWER AND INFLUENCE

One of the characteristics of entrepreneurship that is at once beautiful, maddening, and inevitable is that ideas come and go. A flower you hoped would bloom perennially turns out to be a one-season wonder. Yet when each project, vision, or collaboration runs its course, it offers you the opportunity to revisit those pivotal moments with a broader aperture.

When the shared vision for Coastal Sage Farms collapsed, I waded knee-deep in intricate analyses of my collaborators' chemistry, trying to understand why our whole was significantly *lesser* than the sum of our parts.

However, when I was able to reflect on that episode with the layered experiences of my time in academia and nonprofits, I started to distinguish the contours of a massive pink giraffe that had been in the room the entire time: power.

Three of the partners were part of the project because of ties to one another and to farming, while the fourth partner was . . . the money. Thanks to his capital, we were going to be able to buy a sizable piece of land and essentially repay him over the course of years. Let's just say the financial differences between us did not make for smooth sailing. And as inexperienced people without a refined sense of how to navigate this power differential in partnership, we glossed over the inequities in power and influence to our great disservice—for all four of us.

This story is as old as the hills. I had lived it in my relationship with my conventional farming partner, I witnessed it in the world of academia (where cultural capital was the currency of choice), and it became all too familiar as I built small organizations that often looked to partner with bigger ones.

For anyone who has ever been presented with the opportunity to forge such a partnership, this prospect can be the thing keeping them up at night: on the one hand, access to money and resources; on the other hand, a slippery slope from bad (compromise) to worse (sellout).

Rare is the nonprofit executive director who hasn't wrestled with a suspect donation or a questionable partnership as they stare in the face of a cash flow crisis. I once attended a development conference whose keynote speaker touted the catchphrase, "there isn't tainted money, it's just that t'aint enough." And while I have some issues with this cynical framing, it does underscore the challenge that many face when struggling to resource their visions for the future.

If you have worked in the social sector or raised money in support of a business venture, you are familiar with the challenge of navigating relationships with those who hold the resources. Even with a funder who has a solid self-awareness of the ways that they hold and wield outsized power, the work of resource development requires recipients to parse through "donor speak" for deeper meanings and nuance, as if unlocking a mystery.

Early on in my organizational leadership, as I learned how to raise resources in support of my initiatives, I would consistently make the mistake of taking donors at their word. As those in the social sector know, high-minded language like "we share a common destiny" and "together we transform the world" can be produced and promoted with little consequence. In fact, this kind of rhetoric is to be expected in a sector that promises fundamental changes within society. And yet, because I was just experienced enough to listen but not wise enough to hear, when donors would turn on the rhetoric of "we are in this together," I believed them.

So when I would open an email from someone who had said they were my passionate partner saying, "You do good work, but . . ." or "We have decided to shift our funding priorities, but all the best in your continued good work . . ." I would feel a crushing sense of betrayal. After a few of these experiences—and getting over my simple-minded, angry reactions—I began to see that I would need to develop a better approach to these kinds of relationships. One that would help me ask better questions and be more sober minded in sifting through the rhetoric, so I would be less likely to be faced with those shocks, going forward.

Now before moving on, I want to address a question that you are probably thinking: Is it possible to be in a real relationship and collaboration with a capital partner or donor?

To this I would say that yes, it *is* possible; it is just my experience that it is a very high bar to clear and, if you are in a supplicant role, be very careful. It can also be helpful to remember that people, in general, come and go, and their priorities change. Yes, it has particular implications when it is a funder, but it is not just about power; it is about the importance of setting clear, shared expectations and taking the time, when necessary, to end a partnership well. Hope is important, but it doesn't pay the bills. A clear understanding of the nature of your partnership and the motivations for your collaboration (on both sides) are essential to the pursuit of sustained fundraising success, and a respectful ending to a partnership, if that time comes.

When we dump farming chemicals onto the dirt, we can prop up all kinds of crops, clearing the way for plants to reach sky-high. But those chemicals can't grow soil. Soil only grows with attentive hard work: time + space + relationships.

Infusing money into an organization can lead to soil growth, but without careful attention to time, space, and relationships, it is just as likely to pump up a stalk that is all leaves and shallow roots—destined to topple in any stiff wind or inclement weather.

There's nothing wrong with a take-the-money collaboration, as long as you have taken the time for reflection: Are we equipped to take on this money? What does the funder really expect? What is the context into which this money is being poured? Do we have sufficient trust and clear communication within our organization? Between the identified partners? A "no" on any one of these questions could mean knocking an organization out of its equilibrium, with money catalyzing a crisis rather than accelerating growth.

UNSUSTAINABLE MONEY

I've seen what happens when you jump into a transactional collaboration without an internal look at your organization's soil: one of my organizations took on a large corporate partnership that doubled the size of the budget, only to have them pull out early when it became apparent we did not have the organizational culture or staffing infrastructure to appropriately manage their ever-changing demands.

A plant-based bunch if ever I've seen one, these partners were all about outputs and KPIs to assess the specific impact of our training. Even as we garnered rave reviews from the participants—and the independent impact report triumphantly announced we had touched 712,000 lives—we strained to meet those quantitative demands, sapping our bandwidth that would have been better spent elsewhere, for where we were as a small organization at that time.

It seemed worth it because we could double our budget, initiate exciting long-term planning, and attract future partners. We *thought* we were looking long term. But we hadn't set up the necessary conditions to sustainably support the influx of funds; to keep up with their escalating requests, we had to accelerate the pace of our investments beyond what was financially sound, even spending more than the funding this corporation could cover. We were racing to react when we should have been reflecting.

From a farming perspective, it's as if my partner had asked me to become an iceberg lettuce farm, taken over half my acreage, and asked for more—requiring me to lease another ten-acre farm and contract machinery and labor to handle the overflow—and then started criticizing my crop because the higher-ups wanted identical, pale green, lettuce globes. And then insisted I document the precise nutritional value of each head of lettuce. And said, "Never mind, we don't like your lettuce." That thought experiment takes the edge off the great green bean compromise in chapter 9.

When the funding was terminated early, the recurring costs of those investments became a greater burden, which pulled the organization deep into debt. We struggled to keep it alive, and while it would eventually come back to stasis, it was a grueling period of learning.

There's an element of luck to why my early collaboration with the conventional farmer worked out and this corporate partnership went belly up, where my literal green bean crop grew as planned while my metaphorical iceberg lettuce venture flopped. And of course there are the roles played by my partners: my farming partner wanted a relationship with me as an organic farmer because that was part of his business objectives, while the corporate partner wanted to mold my work to suit their image.

I don't regret having taken the gamble on that corporate partnership; I would do it again today. But I know that had I given more priority to the question of conditions and context, it would have been a different experience. Had I brought on board someone with corporate partnership expertise, instead of thinking I could manage it all myself, we would have been more able to discern and propose the appropriate kind of collaboration. Had we been clearer from the start with this partner about our purpose, boundaries, and expectations, we would have had a more defined framework for discussion with them.

In short, in order to be ready to take on a collaboration of that nature, I not only had to address the intricacies of working with another organization and work to understand their motivations, but I also had to cultivate the conditions within my own organization and for myself as a leader. The tools of inquiry and reflective practice were even more necessary to help bring me to greater clarity on the situation and the challenges we were facing.

What I come away with, time and again, is that trust, respect, and boundaries—*connection*—are the stuff of soil, the essential elements that, over time and with intention, form the foundation for sustainability and, when present, help to mitigate the experiences of short-term failure.

The decision to take the money without addressing the context (on both sides of a collaboration) is like a burst of fertilizer into a field of tomatoes. The application makes the plants grow larger and robust—producing more flowers and fruits—but underneath the surface, the root systems are superficial. The roots of a tomato plant can extend up to three feet into the soil, pushed deeper in the search for nutrients and water, and thus are more resilient in the face of uneven irrigation. But when the plant is being generously fed from the surface, there is little need to cultivate a deeper foundation. Repeat that cycle of dependency long enough, and it can be brutal to watch when the supply is cut off.

When I now reflect on each of the shared-destiny initiatives in my life that came up short, I do not lament their unfulfilled promise but appreciate what this series of experiences taught me about working with others. While I am still moved and animated by emotion, as I was when I envisioned Coastal Sage Farms, this focus on alignment and connection has helped me tremendously in setting strategy and making decisions.

No one wants to tend a crop—for months (or years!)—only to come away with fruitless vines or bug-eaten leaves. But when soil and plant are both in view, when we tend to the conditions *and* what takes root deep within them, we can take the invitation to turn the failed crop back into the soil, and plant something new.

When it comes to the act of collaborating, working together to achieve a common purpose, this approach is foundational. As we've said, the idealized rarely manifests into the realized, and what gets lost in translation is the source of misunderstandings, miscommunications, and missed goals.

A functional, healthy collaboration becomes an ecosystem unto itself. Able to withstand disasters and grow back stronger than ever.

Able to sustain itself with the right amount of effort—effort that feels generative, not draining. Able to adapt and change with minimal disruption.

In this way, you might say that Tolstoy was right about families but wrong about collaborations: the happy ones are all happy in their own special way (sometimes, to outsiders, seemingly mystically and enviably so), but the unhappy ones all can be traced back to the same essential problem—the collaborations filed under unsatisfying and unsuccessful are fundamentally misaligned in terms of understanding what collaboration is and what is necessary to realize its fullest potential. These collaborations start with compacted soil, and instead of getting aerated, it simply hardens.

Navigating Collaborations in Pakistan

"I work in the education sector in Pakistan, and collaboration is integral to my work, involving various stakeholders, such as administrators, teachers, students, and parents. As I navigate these relationships, I have realized that not every partnership has to be transformational, and different relationships possess distinct capacities for deep change. Through the collaborative framework, I understand that in order to effectively engage in collaborations, building awareness of our current position is crucial. Understanding the expectations, contributions, and reciprocation involved helps me to set appropriate goals and acknowledge that relationships and collaborations can exist in multiple realms simultaneously, and their dynamics evolve over time. There is no universal hierarchy or prescribed path for every collaboration. Instead, the strength of a collaboration lies in aligning our rhetoric with reality, making sure our visions are supported by effective execution.

I have also come to appreciate the value of purely transactional collaborations, emphasizing equitable and inclusive interactions. These collaborations can be highly effective in driving progress and fostering positive change. By embracing this understanding of collaboration, I can better approach my work and leadership."

Mateen Sheikh (Pakistan)
Head of Product Development
Taleemabad

Embracing Collaboration in Rwanda

"As a social entrepreneur and advocate for women's empowerment in Rwanda, I've come to realize that collaboration is not just about working side by side, but about leveraging each other's unique talents and resources to achieve a common purpose. At OSO, we recognize that not every relationship has the potential for a deep transformational collaboration. We have become more aware of the parameters and what goes into collaboration and transformed the way we work at OSO. It has allowed us to navigate partnerships more effectively and develop more practical strategies. Collaboration isn't just a buzzword for us; it's a guiding principle that shapes our approach to achieve our vision of ending poverty through education and innovative local solutions."

Delphine Uwamahoro (Rwanda)
Founder and Executive Director
Our Sisters' Opportunity (OSO)

REFLECTION

As you complete this chapter, I invite you to take a moment to pause and reflect on the following inquiries.

- What has been one of your most generative collaborations? Using the collaboration screen, how would you categorize that collaboration? To the best of your ability, list the motivations of each of the participants. Even in the best collaborations, there are misalignments (not all humans think the same way; this is one of the best reasons to collaborate!). Where are the differences and even misalignments? How did those show up in the collaboration?
- What has been one of your most challenging collaborations? Try running this one through the collaboration screen as well. Were the misalignments apparent from the start or did they emerge over time?
- Categorize your current organization's three most important collaborations: where do they fall on the collaboration screen?
- In each collaboration, does the rhetoric match the reality? If not, which needs to be adjusted, rhetoric or lived experience? Don't be afraid to adjust the rhetoric—sometimes a transactional relationship is all you need; just don't pretend it is something else.

CHAPTER 11

Collaborative Inquiry

Sometimes
when I
write,
it
autocorrects to
right.
Good to remember,
we can
change
the settings.

"Why am I staring at a grenade, on the ground in front of me, with the pin pulled?"

This is not a metaphor.

Buried under the matted canopy of layers of weeds gone to seed, there it was.

Could there have been a more evocative and symbolic thing to find on an urban farm seeking to reclaim and rebuild a piece of land to be a place for growth instead of destruction?

Far from the bucolic imaginations of a scripted, performative agriculture, the urban farm—the one set in between housing tracts and twenty-four-hour convenience stores—can feel like a place of constant conflict, where farmers are fighting daily to prove their craft deserves space.

So on that day when I heard the banging around in the tractor's rototiller and stopped to find a grenade with the pin missing, I was not surprised. This was just another part of the story—a multi-year remediation process, during which we would transform this tract of dirt, which had been home to all manner of urban waste, into living, breathing, organic soil. Humans will put anything in the dirt. It was now my job to turn that dirt into soil. Turn it from depleted, cast-off land to generative farm field.

In the early days of that process, we had driven off many a truck load of old tires and their brethren, but we were now at the phase where our work resembled more that of sustainable farmers than trash collectors: building up beds by adding rows of compost, planting cover crops to add nitrogen and other nutrients into the depleted soil, and introducing oxygen into the compacted earth with tools like broadforks.

Although we were nominally past the urban waste phase, knowing the history of this land meant that we could never kick off our shoes for an idyllic toes-in-grass frolic. But it would have taken an imagination more expansive than mine to have anticipated a grenade.

I had never held a grenade before, and for whatever reason, I took a very close look at this one. It was smaller than I would have imagined, more lemon than orange, and although it was covered with dust, the markings made it clear.

Unlike a sustainable farm where one might eventually unearth all the surprises that sit beneath the surface, in leadership the unexpected turn is inherent to the experience.

In leadership there are always going to be grenades outside of our view—which underscores the importance of tilling and turning over the earth.

REFLECTING WITH OTHERS

Individual reflection through Reflective Practice is one way that we surface hidden grenades, but collaborative inquiry is even more effective in exposing our misguided assumptions and gaps in awareness. Remembering the core capacity in leadership introduced in chapter 3, being able to answer the question "What's going on here?" to the best of our abilities, collaborative inquiry, reflection, and discovery ensures that we have more knowledge to work from and, in many cases, a more grounded and aware emotional state from which to operate.

Collective reflection on a specific event can open new pathways for conversation between people and, most importantly, increase awareness and understanding. Reflecting with others is a way to stay in inquiry and slow down the action, so that leaders can better discern and evaluate before moving to forming judgment and taking action. And at a deeper level, all of these more formal, structured approaches to reflection are here to help leaders cultivate the conditions of greater self-awareness and relationship to self.

When we are engaged in this practice together, it is called Collaborative Inquiry.

If Reflective Practice is largely an individual act to gain more clarity regarding the deeper roots of an issue, event, or phenomenon, Collaborative Inquiry is a collective act with a similar purpose: to lift awareness and deepen connection to self, others, and context.

In this chapter I will introduce three core processes in collaborative inquiry that, like the individual Reflective Practice process, you can apply in your work settings.

SOIL-BUILDING CONVERSATIONS

I have learned many things over my time working with leaders and organizations all over the world, but perhaps the most common and straightforward truism—whether you are in Nepal, Nairobi, New Zealand, or Nicaragua—is that we all struggle to have conversations that help participants feel seen and heard and that result in generative outcomes. Because of this, for many years now in my organization's flagship fellowship program for leaders, we have prioritized the practice of what we call "soil-building conversations." These are processes that prioritize connection among participants and effectively cultivate the conditions—build the soil—to bring people closer to each other and generate the kind of safety and security necessary for meaningful connections where we feel seen, heard, and understood.

Sharing

Purpose over Performance and Perfection: We tend to enter conversations with the intent to "say the right thing" or "say it in the right way." It is far more important to get clear on your purpose: why are you sharing what you are sharing? Before you speak, take a few moments to ground yourself and point toward the "why."

Seek Connection: As you speak, prioritize an emotional connection to the receivers. Are you speaking and sharing in such a way that invites and allows for that?

It's Your Time: Many of us struggle to hold and comfortably fill the time we are allotted to speak and share. To promote equity, in our work at Perennial, we often assign equal time for each speaker to speak. At the same time, we do not allow the speaker to give away their time to others. This does not mean that you need to fill the entire time with words, but this form of structure and boundary helps to establish the overall integrity of a process that can generate more meaningful connections.

Silence Is Safe: In many cases, what is communicated in silence is more evocative than any spoken word. When we know that we can be silent, our spoken words can find greater connection to their deeper roots and purpose.

Speak from "I": When we speak using *I statements* (putting ourselves as the subject), something changes in the quality and nature of our conversations. Doing so requires us to take ownership of our thoughts, feelings, and opinions, and it significantly shifts the ways in which we are heard and received.

Receiving

Full Presence: Before you start the conversation, set aside anything that will prevent you from being fully present—physically, mentally, and emotionally. Even if you struggle with asking good questions, providing your full emotional and mental presence for someone who is sharing is a powerful gift that cultivates the conditions for transformational conversations.

Active Listening: Many of us confuse waiting our turn to speak with listening. A Soil-Building Conversation will be most generative when the speaker feels that they are being heard by the receiver(s). Being a good listener means connecting to whatever the speaker is sharing and helping them to find clarity. If you struggle with speaking too much and/or taking up space with your words, it can be helpful to remember to WAIT—which stands for Why Am I Talking?

Hold Uncertainty (no fixing): Your role is not to solve anyone's problems, mentor, or give advice. Instead, work to ground yourself in a way that accompanies the speaker on a journey of discovery through their own uncertainty. This is achieved by asking open, honest questions that can help them find their own clarity and resourcefulness. You are not there to provide the answer but to seek clarity in partnership with the one who is sharing.

Stay Curious (good questions vs. giving advice): Listen with an open mind to others' truth. This is not about assessing who is right and who is wrong. Turn from reaction and judgment toward reflection and inquiry. Ask "I wonder why they feel/think this way?" versus "How can I explain to them that they are wrong?"

Practice Confidentiality: When we can trust that our words and stories will remain within the boundaries of the conversation, it creates the conditions for sharing and transformation. Conversely, if we fear that our open-hearted sharing will travel to places beyond the realm of our informed consent, we will remain closed. The words and stories you receive are those of the sharer. Hold them gently and respect their origin.

Timekeeping: Time can be a very important structure and boundary for conversations. If you have a limited time frame, it is important to honor and keep track of the timing. If possible, assign the role of a timekeeper to let the speaker know how much time they have.

REFLECTION AND DISCOVERY CIRCLE

Another collaborative inquiry approach that has proved to be useful in my work with leaders is the Reflection and Discovery Circle (RDC). The RDC is a collective form of Reflective Practice that seeks to generate more clarity in understanding the complex systems that surround our personal and organizational lives, and it can lead to a greater awareness of our relationships and a larger perspective on leadership and decision-making. The RDC process follows a relatively strict set of guidelines, but it is not overly complicated and can be used both in-person and virtually. At its core, the RDC is a collective, collaborative discernment tool that helps to surface and unearth the grenades that live in all our soils and contexts.

Head to the Soil of Leadership website to download the RDC worksheet, which details the step-by-step process; however, there are some important points to note and reinforce when doing a Reflection and Discovery Circle.

- There should be at least two Peer Consultants. Two or three is a great number. Anything more than four can be cumbersome.

- Be sure to review the principles of Soil Building Conversations before the process begins. Even if you are very familiar with the principles, a quick review can help reground you in your role and how you can best participate.
- For the entirety of the RDC, if all participants can offer their full presence (close all other screens and tabs, silence phones, etc.), it will go a long way in making the RDC a success.
- Stay true to the timings—the limiting structures of the RDC are a big part of what make it an effective (and efficient) tool. All the timings are carefully calibrated and informed by years of iteration and learning by doing.
- Don't skip over the quiet reflection!
- At first, it will be unfamiliar, if not a bit uncomfortable, for the Peer Consultants to speak to each other as if the Presenter was not in the room. But it is critical that you do this, as the Presenter can learn a great deal from just listening to how the Peer Consultants are making sense of the Presenter's issue.
- For Peer Consultants—remember that your role is *not* to provide advice but to help ask powerful questions that help the Presenter come to their own greater clarity. Peer Consultants may need to keep each other in check on this matter, as so many of us (particularly if we are in positions of influence and authority) default to this form (advice giving) of participation. If you find yourself beginning a sentence with "You should . . ." then maybe reconsider your contribution. An example of this might be where a Presenter is bringing forward to the group a challenge with an employee.
    - » Advice Based (no): "You should be firmer with them and tell them if they don't change their behavior, they will lose their job."

    - Inquiry Based (yes!): "What do you think would motivate this employee to improve their performance?"
- Don't forget that the learning from the experience is not only for the Presenter, but also for the Peer Consultants.
- When it is over, it is over—which is to say, after the reflection has been completed, consider the RDC closed.

While all of this may feel like a lot to coordinate, an RDC is something that can be easily done in one hour and either in person or virtually. While the Presenter should come prepared, the Peer Consultants only need to be familiar with the methodology and the principles of Soil Building Conversations.

Try it out and see what you can collectively create.

COLLECTIVE REFLECTIVE PRACTICE

Another approach to collaborative inquiry is rather simple and builds on what we introduced earlier with Reflective Practice. In Collective Reflective Practice, when a group of people experience a similar event, they all complete the Reflective Practice outline, then later come together and share their learnings. It may sound basic, but the learnings from the experience can be remarkable; often the conversations bring people closer together, thus strengthening bonds and cultivating the conditions for transformation—soil building—that we have been discussing. It is also a very clear illustration of how we all see things from different perspectives—even with events where it might seem like we all saw the same thing. When this exercise is coupled with the principles of Soil Building Conversations, we find that this is the very stuff of empathetic and compassionate leadership, as people hear how others make sense of a familiar event in their own unique ways. This approach can be particularly helpful when something happens in the workplace that is difficult and divisive. When these things happen (and they always do), a key question for leaders is how to reconnect people to each other. I have found that this approach to collaborative inquiry is one of the most effective ways to do this very thing.

Engaging in Collective Reflective Practice

- Agree on who will be participating in the process and what the event will be that anchors the reflection. The number of participants can be anywhere from two on up.
- Be sure to review the principles of Soil Building Conversations before the process begins. Even if you are very familiar with the principles, a quick review can help reground you in your role and how you can best participate.
- There is no strict rule(s) around how you will share your learning(s) from individually doing the Worksheet. I have found it effective both when participants share their worksheets with each other prior to a collective conversation and also when there is no prior sharing, and it is just the collective conversation.
- Before you begin your collective conversation, it can be helpful to first get clear on the "why" of the conversation: what you are hoping to get out of the conversation, how you will proceed, and with what process.

Collaborative Inquiry is important not because we *might* find a grenade in our soil, but so that we *can*.

Soil building is and should be an ongoing process, one that requires us to be adaptive and dynamic as we do the work of identifying, discerning, and addressing the myriad challenges inherent in leading teams, organizations, and businesses. While many of us may wish for predictability, leadership is not a convergent activity where we come to a point of permanence and stability, but rather the opposite, where divergence and the tenuous and fleeting nature of clarity rule the day.

Learning Together in Kenya

"Collaborative Inquiry is one of the most valuable approaches that I use with my team. At Hatua we help youth in Mombasa enter the workforce and lift themselves out of poverty. Like most organizations, we regularly experience events that require careful processing, but struggle with how to do so. I have been amazed at how differently we all experience the same event, and these tools have given us the space to share diverse perspectives and to be more expansive. It has proven to be critical in our growth and evolution."

Peter Kwame Mwakio (Kenya)
Cofounder and Director
Hatua Network

Discovering Together in Central America

"While individual reflection has helped uncover hidden insights, engaging in a collective reflection has taken our understanding to new heights. Initially, our team had a hard time sticking to the time frame, but as we continued to use the structure, we got more clear and have been able to identify areas for improvement, refine our approach, and make informed decisions as a team. It has been so important in uncovering hidden assumptions and, time after time, leads to a more comprehensive and informed solution."

Marlon Velasquez (Nicaragua/Honduras)
National Director
Nuestros Pequeños Hermanos

REFLECTION

As you complete this chapter, I invite you to take a moment to pause and reflect on the following inquiries.

- Generally speaking, how well do you and your team(s) communicate with each other? How would you describe the quality of your conversations?
- Have you or your team ever used structures such as the Soil Building Conversations process? If so, what have you learned from using formal conversation structures? Has the commitment to using these structures been maintained? Why or why not?

- Have you recently surfaced any hidden "grenades" in your work? How did you identify them, and what did you do as a result of discovering them?
- Can you think of two upcoming meetings or projects for which you can use the Collaborative Inquiry and Reflection and Discovery Circle tools?

CONCLUSION

百姓

Words, like material objects, can fall out of use and into disrepair. The contexts in which they are born evolve, and so do the meanings and associations. So it is with the traditional word for farmer in Japanese, a word that continues to resonate, some twenty-five years after first hearing it on Dr. Takekuma's farm, acting as a touchstone for how I see myself and my approach to leadership.

The word is *hyakusho.*

Unlike most Western-alphabet language systems, Japanese words maintain both phonetic and symbolic representations. These symbolic representations are illustrated in the use of *kanji* (Chinese characters), which can be said in different ways, depending on context, but hold their symbolic meaning irrespective of pronunciation. In the case of the word *hyakusho,* there are two kanji: the first being 百 (hyaku), which means one hundred, and the second 姓 (sho), which can be broadly defined as talents or skills. So, put together, the *hyakusho* was the one with a hundred talents—not a surprise given all of the things that need tending on a farm.

There are many reasons why a word can lose favor, but in the case of *hyakusho*, it is likely to have come up against the kind of condescension and discrimination directed at rural folk around the world—seeing them as backward or premodern peasants, underprepared to succeed in a modern economy. The twentieth century in Japan was an era of modernization projects, with business and industry leading the way to urbanize and raise the country's influence on the global economy. Now farmers are typically called ファマ (fa-mah), using katakana, the syllabic Japanese script primarily used for words of foreign origin, or 農家 (noka), which can be translated as "family of the field."

No one uses *hyakusho* anymore to describe a farmer, and in fact, it could be perceived as an insult to do so. Using the language of this book, it could be said that the word *hyakusho* has become associated with dirt, when its deeper meaning is of the soil.

But the word offers more than just a beautiful reclamation story. In fact, I believe that it speaks to the kind of leaders we need more of today.

Leaders, like the *hyakusho,* who have countless talents and flexible skills to address their needs and fulfill their purpose. Leaders who recognize the complexity of the worlds they inhabit and understand that they are not the center of the action but a conduit of energy, unifying the separated elements in their ecosystems to foster growth and transformation. Leaders who understand the kind of hard work and challenges that go into production and creation but who seek the generative, expansive power that comes as a result of the pursuit.

Leaders who are prepared to reflect, discern, and discover how to better align their intent and impact.

And the practice of being adaptive, nimble, and responsive to change is the very stuff of resilience. Not the problematic version of resilience that conflates it with strength, endurance, and cruel levels of carrying capacity.

But the kind of resilience that comes from regenerative agriculture—a resilience that is a positive, generative outcome of living soil and deep roots rather than a behavior of last resort in response to great suffering and pain.

The *hyakusho* turns the dirt into soil.

CONDITIONS MATTER

When I think about that formative time, farming with Dr. Takekuma in Japan, even if I wanted to take what I was doing there and apply it or transplant it unadjusted into a US context, the conditions were radically different. And if I am being honest, I failed to understand the challenge of transference, and that was one major reason why I left the farming profession. Ultimately, it was not for lack of good intentions nor a clear purpose. I had failed to understand that the conditions—the soil—were not there to support the kind of impact I believed I could have.

And that's okay.

This realization reminds us that conditions matter, and they are sometimes such that your interventions and strong intent to improve things won't result in you achieving your vision.

And I'm here to say: do it anyway.

The Soil of Leadership is not intended to live in a rarefied air of perfection where anything less than the ideal outcomes is deemed failure. It recognizes that leadership is complicated, hard, messy work that can become transformational for both you and the people you work with when you are more deeply rooted in purpose, fed by well-being, and connected to what matters.

Model, Adapt, Teach Others, Adjust

The work of the Soil of Leadership is not something to keep for yourself; it is, of course, about relationships and about sharing these insights with others. To maintain your soil building practices and to develop them in partnership with others, the acronym MATA (Model, Adapt, Teach Others, Adjust) may be helpful to remember as you move forward.

Model: firstly, it is important that you shift this learning from the realm of concept (the intellect) to the realm of application. Rather than *tell* others about how important these concepts might be, *show* them.

Adapt: second, just as a seed variety adapts to its new conditions, the learning from this book should also be adapted to your unique context.

Teach Others: by meaningfully engaging the steps of Model and Adapt, you can prepare yourself to teach others. Once you have embodied and internalized the learnings in ways that are appropriate to your soil context, it will be easier to teach and train others.

Adjust: finally, this is a reminder that these ideas and concepts are always going to be open for improvement and change as you apply them.

GERMINATION

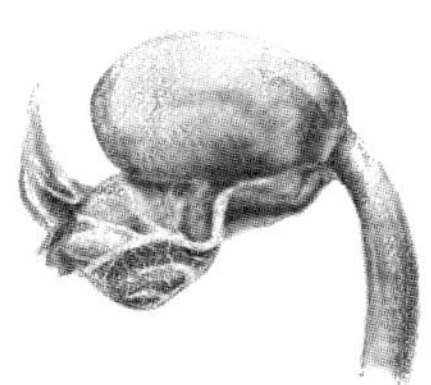

When a seed has absorbed just enough moisture and heat to soften, swell, and show its new face to the world.

When the doorway to sentience has opened, and the passage from dormancy to wakefulness, vulnerable and full of promise, has begun.

When new shapes and configurations emerge.

We have germination.

Germination is about what can be.

Germination is about what lies ahead.

Germination is hope.

We speak of how the spring light grows, warms the earth, and summons green shoots to feed in its glow. That hope, transformed into visible action, growth, and progress. We speak of how "hope springs eternal" and could just as easily reassemble the words to "spring's eternal hope" and evoke the same sentiment.

Green shoots, rising above the soil line.

This is the promise of life fulfilled, yet with the potential for even greater outcomes.

Germination is hope.

But while it is the green shoot that captures our attention and represents the potential of leaders to create and grow their initiatives, I invite you to draw closer to the other actor, overshadowed by the showy bud bending toward the light: that is, the unassuming, tiny, first root that snakes out of the seed husk and finds its way into the loamy earth.

Here, the first shoot is about potential, but the first root is about purpose.

As leaders, we need the presence of both.

While it feels good to be moved by inspiration and possibility, the Soil of Leadership reminds us that in the absence of substance and intent, our leadership will remain in the realm of superficiality and cannot fully reach the depth of its potential.

I used to believe that leadership was mostly about charisma and inspiring growth in others.

But I have come to realize through my own failures and learnings that without a clear commitment to the rootedness of being, the soil building in self and for others, such leadership is hollow and performative at best, and manipulative and toxic at its worst.

So let us celebrate the activated potential in germination, but let us remember that healthy and strong root growth is what drives the realization of potential.

It is the hidden and inner world, outside of the view of many, that shapes our presentation in leadership.

The deeper the roots, the stronger the shoots.

Seasons

Our lives,
like the seasons,
turn from light
into darkness.
The warmth of the sun
shrinks
into the horizon.
Green falls brown
to the
ground,
here to nourish
and renew.
Shapes and sizes,
failures, success,
scars,
celebrations.
Let them fall.
Let them be
free,
metabolized,
transformed
into
something new.
From
the darkness
comes the
light.
From
your roots,
the way
found.
From
the soil,
your purpose
reborn,
again.

ACKNOWLEDGMENTS

The fruits of *The Soil of Leadership* owe their existence to the deep roots and fertile earth of the loving contributions, insights, and encouragement from Mariko, Marisa, Jennifer, Kaia, Priti, Don, Karen, Douglas, Isao, Takami, Sawyer, Tarsha, JB, Russ, Neil, Margarita, and the countless participants who have inspired me along this journey. Your unwavering support and belief have been my driving force. Thank you.

A heartfelt appreciation goes out to Izumi, without whom I would have never developed a sense of clarity and greater understanding of myself and my leadership.

ABOUT THE AUTHOR

Dr. Britt Yamamoto is a visionary leader, entrepreneur, and educator with over two decades of experience shaping inclusive and generative learning environments across diverse sectors. As a clinical associate professor at the University of Washington's Department of Global Health, and the founding force behind international leadership organizations such as Perennial, RootSpring, and SOIL, he has ignited the leadership potential within hundreds of thousands of individuals worldwide, from India to Iraq, Malawi to Mexico, and Cambodia to Canada. His transformative influence extends to nurturing deeper connections with one's work, partnerships, and self.

With a PhD in geography, an MSc in community development, and a wealth of experience leading organizations and managing people, Britt's technical and practical expertise is evident. However, his unique approach to leadership development is deeply rooted in a range of interests that contribute to his holistic well-being. A creature of the Pacific, you are likely to find him engaged in endurance athletics, savoring memorable meals with family and friends, exploring the surface and depths of oceans, sifting through used vinyl, and searching for the perfect taco.

Join Britt on a journey of transformation, where leadership and personal growth converge to illuminate and create a more hopeful, generative, and connected world.